Loving Your Husband Before You Even Have One

KIM VOLLENDORF

HIGH BRIDGE
BOOKS & MEDIA

ISBN: 978-1-962802-54-3
LCCN: 2017959415

5 6 7 8 9 10 11 12 13 14   Printing/Year 25 24 23 22 21

What Single Women Are Saying About
Loving Your Husband Before You Even Have One

Kim has poured her whole heart into this book, and that is what makes *Loving Your Husband Before You Even Have One* so special. Hearing from someone who has actually felt the same feelings we feel, but now has clear hindsight is refreshing and provides hope. Each reader will walk away feeling like she has been heard and understood. For me, I now know that there is hope for a happy marriage, I know practical steps to take in learning to love my husband before I even have one, and I know about my worth in our sweet Savior. —*Madison*

I never considered my single years as a privilege or a time of preparation. I never thought I could be actively taking steps to love my husband before I even have one. This book changed my mind, and I know my relationship with the Lord and with those around me will thrive because of it! —*McKenna*

At an age where many of my friends are getting married, I can truly celebrate them without being filled with the bitterness and jealousy I once had. Through this book I have learned how to maximize my single years and be thankful for this time God is giving me to learn how to love my husband before I even have one. —*Deven*

Kim helped me realize how much my decisions now will impact my future love life. This book is full of practical, relatable advice from an author who sincerely cares about the women who will read it. Applying the wisdom provided here has impacted every relationship I have.
—*Cymber*

I'm so glad I came across Kim's book when I did. Her book truly helped me revive faith, understand the importance of godly relationships, and was the jumpstart to a new way of living. I learned a lot through Kim's vulnerable stories. Her book is easy to read and full of noteworthy advice.
—*Amy*

What Married Women Are Saying About
Loving Your Husband Before You Even Have One

Kim and Sean have invested in and influenced my marriage more than anyone else on earth, and we owe so much to them. To have her wisdom in book form is GOLD. I am so excited to have this resource to give young women. —*Sarah*

Be ready for your heart to be filled with hope. —*Brenda*

The second most important decision you will make in life, aside from following Christ, is choosing your spouse. It really is your choice, and the things I learned in the chapter *Choosing Wisely* saved me from making the greatest mistake and settling for less in a spouse. —*Hannah*

I wish *Loving Your Husband Before You Even Have One* would have been available when I was in college. —*Kara*

Kim has helped countless single and married women over the years to love God and experience Christ-centered relationships. I'm so thrilled that she packaged her best thoughts in *Loving Your Husband Before You Even Have One*. Ladies, go grab this book! —*Brooke*

Page in and page out, this book challenged me to look beyond the normal ways the world does love—beyond tv shows, friends, advice and even my own experiences and attempt to understand God's design for us as women and as future wives! —*Megan*

I love how Kim unpacks these timeless principles that can benefit any relationship! The chapter on forgiveness is powerful. The truths presented have been a huge blessing for me and my marriage. —*Amber*

This book is a MUST read for women in this generation desiring happy, healthy marriages that last! —*Macie*

What Leaders are Saying About
Loving Your Husband Before You Even Have One

Kim's voice is a comforting source of wisdom as you sort through the maze of dating, sexuality, and finding true love!
— *Dr. Juli Slattery, Authentic Intimacy*

We met Kim when she was in college and have been privileged to watch her dating engagement, and marriage unfold. In this book, Kim is vulnerable, honest, and practical as she encourages young women to prepare for the life choices ahead! A must read for any young woman!
— *Steve and Carol Shadrach, Center for Mission Mobilization*

In her relationship with her husband, both before and after God gave him to her, Kim has lived out the biblical principles she humbly presents for the good of all women and the glory of God.
— *Julia Robinson, Retired Bible Study Fellowship Teaching Leader*

This book is a must read for every young woman who wants a "happily ever after" of her own! — *Tonya Zunigha, Faith Bible Church*

I talk to so many college girls around the country who want to be used by God in big ways. BUT they don't realize that their dating and relationship habits have the potential to derail those hopes more than almost anything else in their lives. I would hand every one of them Kim's book. Her wisdom and practical advice will help any girl dramatically improve her chances of a long-lasting, satisfying, and God-glorifying marriage. — *Jessie Smith, The Traveling Team*

I was lucky enough to know Kim while I was in college, and she began teaching me some ways I could love my husband before I ever had one. I can't wait to put this book into the hands of every college woman I know.
— *Meagan Shearin, Campus Outreach*

To the young women
who overflowed my workshops at SMC 2014, 2015, and 2016

and to Sean,
because I want each one of them to marry a man like you

What Kim's husband has to say about
Loving Your Husband Before You Even Have One

I'll never forget the first time I met Kim Graves. I was preparing to speak to a group of college students. She was planning the program and needed to know how to pronounce my last name. She struggled a bit to say it. Ironic since it's now hers. Even though I was blown away by her beauty and the sweet, confident way she carried herself, it never occurred to me to ask her out. I was 19. She was 26. I was 5'11." She was 6'1." I was a boy. She was a woman.

Even though I didn't see her for a couple of years, I would hear stories about the way she lived her life. She was a hard worker, a quiet influencer, a beautiful spirit, a faithful friend. Even though I noticed other girls, Kim became the standard by which I would judge every other young lady I met.

Years later, when we finally dated and married, I felt incredibly fortunate to be the man who married Kim Graves. I still do. On a daily basis, she sees my flaws, and I see hers. But I'm regularly amazed by how kind, consistent, unselfish, hardworking, and empathetic she is. Almost daily, I think about the years she spent preparing to love me the way she does. She worked hard and truly learned to love me before she met me. And because of that, I absolutely love my life.

I'm always telling single guys, "If you want to know what kind of woman to marry, come to my home for dinner. Watch how my wife lives her life, and then marry someone like her." I've been telling them that for twenty years. You're going to love reading this book. Like a lot of books, it will challenge and encourage you. Like far fewer books, the author actually lives what she's going to ask you to live. I know. I see it every day. May God bless you as you go on this journey of loving your husband before you even have one.

Sean Vollendorf

Contents

...and they lived happily ever after.

—Every love story ever written

Introduction

Happily Ever After?

We sat there side by side, staring out opposite windows. The music drifting through the speakers wasn't enough to overpower the eerie silence that filled my car. I felt colder than normal so I pulled my jacket tighter around my shoulders. I couldn't believe that we had come to this, but too much had changed for us to try to stay the same.

Taking a deep breath, I finally broke the silence and said to my fiancé, "I think we should break up." We had been working through some issues so this did not come as a total shock, but he could not understand why we had to completely end our relationship. I tried to explain my reasons, but they weren't making any sense to him. His breathing became slower and deeper. He was getting angry. "Just give the ring back to my parents," he said. Then he got out of the car and slammed the door.

This wasn't how I imagined my happily ever after. Ever since I was a little girl, I had hoped to find the man of my dreams, be swept off my feet in romance, and walk down the aisle in wedded bliss. I thought my plan was falling into place, but we never even made it to the altar. As I watched him walk out into the night, I began to sob, snot and all, as my happily ever after came to a heartbreaking end.

Relationships were harder than I thought they would be.

Relationships were harder than I thought they would be. How is it that they can be so wonderful at the beginning but often end so horribly wrong?

How are your relationships?

"Uh, what relationship?"

"I'm with a guy I really like, but how do I know if he's 'the one'?"

"I've done my share of snot-crying. Next time I will know what kind of guy to avoid. I won't make that mistake again."

"Oh, I'm so over relationships. They aren't worth the pain. I'm just reading this book because my friend told me to."

"I'd rather just hook up and avoid the messy relationship stuff altogether."

"Marriage is the furthest thing from my mind right now. Why are we even talking about it?"

Here's why I'm talking about it. If a lasting, enjoyable marriage is something you want someday, sadly the odds are against you. You may not be able to tell from the relationships forming around you right now, but not many marriages make it. These headlines don't paint a very promising picture of happily ever after:

Why Are So Many People in an Unhappy Marriage?[1]

More People Say They're Unhappy in Their Marriages Than Ever Before[2]

It's Time to Accept This Fact: A Really Great Marriage Is Rare[3]

Most in U.S. Want Marriage, but Its Importance Has Dropped[4]

Perhaps this is a good time to tell you the rest of my story.

Twelve years after the fateful night at the park, a friend named Sean asked me to have dinner with him. By then I was in my thirties, and I was accepting the idea that my happily ever after might not include marriage. That dinner date, however, set our friendship on a track for something more, and it didn't take long to realize that Sean was the one I'd been hoping for all along. Our relationship not only made it to the altar, but after twenty years of marriage we are still crazy about each other.

So, what was different between these two relationships? Why did one end in heartbreak and one continues to thrive? What changed?

I changed.

I became different.

And the crazy thing is, I have my single years to thank for it.[5]

Being single was never, ever part of my original plan. However, after my first engagement ended, it's what I was given, year after year after year. When everyone around me started getting married, I was asked to be a bridesmaid in their weddings. Thirteen of them. *Thirteen.*

Looking back, my single years were great, but at the time I didn't want them. As I was bemoaning the fact that every girl around me was falling in love and finding the happiness I yearned for, God was providing opportunities for me to learn and grow as a person. I gained valuable wisdom and skills that have really paid off in life. Silly me. While I was forcing the "happy for you" bridesmaid smile, thinking God was cheating me out of my own love and happiness, the reality was He was blessing my life that entire time! God used my single years to develop me. He built my character, changed my perspective, increased my abilities, and strengthened my friendships. He grew me into a stronger, more confident woman.

What if you intentionally used your single years to start preparing yourself now for the relationship you hope to have someday?

My single years made me a better me. Because of that, I am convinced that I would have had a happily ever after whether I had married or not. But having married, I can say with confidence that along with making me a *better me*, my single years also gave me a *better marriage*.

Statistics say that most young women still hope to get married someday.[6] Well if that's the case, I have a crazy idea for you. What if you intentionally used your single years to start preparing yourself *now* for the relationship you hope to have *someday*?

It's kinda like you are loving your husband *before* you even have one.

I have written for you the book I wish I could have read when I was single. Had I understood the lifelong value of what I was learning back then, I am certain I would have relaxed and actually enjoyed my single years more. The things I learned about life, about God, and about myself when I was single helped me build a better happily ever after. I think they can help you too.

Over the years I've seen a lot of marriages fall apart, and I've cried alongside many women. When I watch marriages break up around me and people I care for hurting in their relationships, I want to somehow help. Sadly, in many instances the damage is done, and the marriage seems beyond repair.

Broken marriages are hard to *repair*, but I began to wonder if maybe I could use my background in mentoring young women to help *prepare* the future ones. I was in a position to help young women get ready for the realities of marriage, empowering them with the knowledge and skills to avoid potential heartbreak and build a lasting, enjoyable relationship.

One day I scribbled down on an index card the key lessons I learned as a single woman that really paid off in marriage. The notes on that card became a series of talks, and I have given those talks to thousands of single women. The response to them blew me away. Young women began to make better choices early on in their relationships because they understood what an enjoyable marriage would require. They liked the idea of loving their husbands ahead of time, and they started preparing themselves to beat the dismal odds.

Just for the record, most marriages have struggles, including my own. Even after two decades, Sean and I are still learning how to love each other well. Unfortunately there is no formula or checklist that guarantees a perfect relationship. But I am still convinced there are some things a girl can do to increase her odds for an enjoyable, lasting marriage, even before she has one.

Gary Chapman, author of *The Five Love Languages* and mentioned in *TIME* magazine as the country's most successful marriage therapist, said in his book, *Things I Wish I'd Known Before We Got Married*:

> *The decision to get married will impact one's life more*
> *deeply than almost any decision in life.*
> *Yet people continue to rush into marriage*
> *with little or no preparation for*
> *making a marriage successful.*[7]

Preparing and acquiring skills are common sense for most of the dreams we have in life. To prepare for our career, we do all kinds of things beforehand to create a great résumé. We pay a lot of money for degrees and carve out years of our life preparing for our dream job. But when it comes to our dream marriage, we often wing it and make one of the most important decisions in life based on feelings and chance. Dr. Chapman points out,

> *Divorce is the lack of preparation for marriage and the*
> *failure to learn the skills of working together*
> *as teammates in an intimate relationship.*[8]

The key to a lasting, enjoyable relationship is rooted in *getting prepared* and *learning skills.*

Many couples value preparation, but they wait until they get engaged to work on their skills. Sean and I have counseled numerous couples as they prepared for marriage.

I've noticed, however, that when couples are starry-eyed in love and distracted by planning a wedding, it is a difficult time to have a crash course in resolving conflict or managing money. So I ask, "Why wait?" The skills I'm referring to can easily be developed when you are single. I know, because that's when I learned them.

Marriage may be far from your mind right now. Just *talking* to a guy or having a *thing* with someone may be all you're looking for. School or work may be taking so much time, guys aren't even on your radar. But somewhere down the line, some guy you meet may change your mind about relationships and marriage. And when that time comes, I want you to know if he's the best one for you, and I want you to be ready if he is.

The way I see it, here are your options when it comes to your future marriage:

Option A: Keep doing what everyone else is doing in relationships and cross your fingers, hoping that your relationship will somehow beat the odds.

Option B: Learn what makes an enjoyable, lasting relationship and start preparing yourself to increase your odds to have one.

Which one sounds best to you?

If you are leaning toward Option B, I'm glad you are here. You are holding in your hands the best of what I've learned. I wholeheartedly believe you can love your husband before you even have one by getting prepared and developing the skills that make a marriage enjoyable and lasting.

You can build a better happily ever after by the choices you make today as a single woman. There's a verse in the Bible that says, "A wise woman builds her home, but a foolish woman tears it down with her own hands."[9] Our choices as women—wise or foolish—affect our homes. I want to share with you wise decisions that will help build your *future* home well. In this adventure of building wisely, I hope you will discover a great deal of strength, creativity, and skills you never dreamed you could have.

Not long after my first engagement broke apart, a friend sat down beside me and asked, "Aww, Kim, why did you guys break up?" I sighed and said, "You know, it just wasn't working out. I think God has a better way of doing relationships, and I am going to find out how to do them."

I found out how, and I came back to share it with you.

You can love your husband, before you even have one, by preparing yourself now for the marriage you'd like to have someday.

Key Truth
A wise woman builds her home, but a foolish woman tears it down with her own hands. Proverbs 14:1

Points to Ponder
If you are a single woman and a lasting, enjoyable marriage is something you want someday, what have you done up to this point to prepare for it?

Action Step
Keep reading. We've got a lot to talk about.

Endnotes

1. Wevorce, "Why are So Many People in an Unhappy Marriage," https://www.wevorce.com/blog/why-are-so-many-people-in-an-un-happy-marriage/ (January 9,2017).

2. Zahra Barnes, "More People Say They're Unhappy in Their Marriages Than Ever Before," *Women's Health*, July 8, 2015, http://www.women-shealthmag.com/sex-and-love/more-are-unhappy-in-their-marriage-than-ever-before.

3. Danielle Teller, "It's Time to Accept This Fact: A Really Great Marriage Is Rare," *Quartz*, August 24, 2014, https://qz.com/254477/its-time-to-accept-this-fact-a-really-great-marriage-is-rare/.

4. Frank Newport and Joy Wilke, "Most in U.S. Want Marriage, but Its Importance Has Dropped," *Gallup News*, August 2, 2013, http://www.gallup.com/poll/163802/marriage-importance-dropped.aspx.

5. Just to clarify, when I talk about my single years, I'm referring to the time when I wasn't married. I had a few boyfriends here and there during this season, but I wasn't married. So, as we move forward together in this book, even if you have a boyfriend, I'm considering you a single woman.

6. Joe S. McIlhaney, Jr., MD and Freda McKissic Bush, MD with Stan Guthrie, *Girls Uncovered: New Research on What America's Sexual Culture Does to Young Women* (Chicago: Northfield Publishing, 2011), 12.

7. Gary Chapman, *Things I Wish I'd Known Before We Got Married* (Chicago: Northfield Publishing, 2010), 10.

8. Chapman, 10.

9. Proverbs 14:1.

I think a lot of girls my age fall into the trap
of thinking that they "love" a guy
or a guy "loves" them after a few dates.
I also think that so many girls just want to feel like
someone loves and cares about them, and they try to
find it in any guy that shows the slightest bit of interest.
—**Alex, nineteen years old**

———————

All I want in life is love. I've wanted it for so long.
—**Caila, The Bachelor, season 20**

1

Spot the Fakes

Find True Love

Like most young women, I spent a lot of time looking
for love. The crazy thing is that I finally found it in a
very unexpected place.

I'd never been to a Bible study before, but my roommate
in the sorority house kept inviting me to go with her. I
wasn't anti-Bible or anything, but the Bible seemed old and
irrelevant. Attending meetings focused on the Bible just
wasn't a priority to me. Besides, I was a *very busy* college
student. As an active member of my sorority, I was on our
intramural bowling team, and we bowled on the same night
as the Bible study, so I couldn't go.

My roommate, however, was undeterred by my faithful
bowling commitment and kept reminding me about it each
week. Then, on one night when we weren't bowling, the
Bible study group met downstairs in the living room of *our*

sorority house. I was left without an excuse. I grabbed the token, dusty Bible I kept on my shelf and sauntered my way down the front stairs. I plopped down on the carpeted floor and attended my first Bible study.

I wasn't sure what to expect. I recognized a couple of familiar faces from some of the other fraternities and sororities on campus. They were all friendly, and a few of the Sigma Chis were making people laugh. I felt pretty comfortable around everyone.

After we hung out and talked for a bit, a guy named Steve stood up to speak. I watched as people began to pull out paper to take notes. I awkwardly did the same. I remember noticing the Bible Steve had was all torn around the edges and loose pages were sticking out. *How did his Bible get in such bad shape?* It never crossed my mind that it was from using it so much.

His topic for the evening, "Looking for Love," redirected my attention away from his worn-out Bible. During the next half hour he described three kinds of love.

I love you if...

"I love you if" is an earned love. In order to get and keep this kind of love, you have to meet certain requirements. It's love with strings attached. If you don't do what's expected, you don't get the love. It's actually quite selfish, because it only gives if it can take. It's the type of love that's focused on what it can get from you. Although it may look like love, it's actually a cheap substitute. It is fake love.

I love you because...

This love is given because of something you are, have, or do. You can have this type of love as long as you maintain the desired quality. Often a person will love another because of their physical appearance, because it makes them look good to be with someone who looks good. "If we are loved because of our looks," Steve asked, "then what happens when someone better looking comes along?" This kind of love produces insecurity, comparison, and jealousy. It is quite selfish as well, because it's focused on what it gets from you. It's also fake love.

But then he mentioned a different kind of love.

I love you regardless...

This type of love is completely different from the other two. It's not earned or deserved. It is a secure love that says, "I will love you no matter what." Unlike the other kinds of love, this love is based on a commitment rather than feelings. "Love if" and "love because" can change as feelings change, but "love regardless" commits to love even when love is not deserved or returned. It's a difficult type of love to give, but it is what everyone, deep down, longs for. It's the kind of love God has for us. It's TRUE love.

He asked us to take a look at the description of love in the Bible in 1 Corinthians 13. I flipped past Genesis and a lot of other books, the names of which I'd never heard of. *Where in the world is Corinthians?* I tried to look like I knew what I was doing. *Wait, there are TWO of them?* Eventually, I found 1 Corinthians. *Well, what do you know?* There it was. This love passage was right there in my Bible, and it had been there all along. I was surprised that the Bible talked so practically about love. *Who knew?*

The Truth about Love from 1 Corinthians 13[1]

True love is patient.
It doesn't lose heart with difficult people and difficult situations.

True love is kind.
It treats people better than they deserve.

True love is not jealous.
It doesn't get resentful when someone else gets something good.

True love is not boastful.
It doesn't draw attention to itself.

True love is not proud.
It isn't focused on its own worth or achievements.

True love isn't rude.
It doesn't disregard the feelings of others.

True love does not demand its own way.
It doesn't put its own needs ahead of the needs of others.

True love is not irritable.
It's not quick to become angry or annoyed.

True love keeps no record of being wronged.
It doesn't play the victim.

True love does not rejoice about injustice, but rejoices whenever the truth wins out.
It celebrates when others choose what is good.

True love never gives up.
It keeps going forever.

True love never loses faith.
It chooses to believe the best about others.

True love is always hopeful.
It sees the potential in people.

True love endures through every circumstance.
It keeps doing the right thing even when it's hard.

As Steve described this kind of love from the Bible, I began to understand that true love encompassed so much more than I had ever realized. You know how people say, "God is love"?[2] Well, it's because God is all of the things that "true love" is in 1 Corinthians 13. God alone perfectly demonstrates all of these qualities of love all of the time. God's love for us is based on who He is, not anything we do to earn or deserve it. That's why we can only find love in its "truest form" in a relationship with God.

Even though God is the only one capable of loving perfectly, He shows us what true love looks like and asks us to follow His example:

This is my commandment:
Love each other in the same way I have loved you.[3]

Loving someone the way that God loves us requires making hard choices to put the other person's needs ahead of our own. "Love regardless" means loving someone even when they aren't particularly loveable. Because we are all selfish, we aren't always going to feel like making the hard, selfless choices that true love requires. That's why true love requires commitment, not just feelings. Loving feelings can come and go, but what distinguishes "love regardless" from "love if" and "love because" is a commitment to love the way God loves us.

I left the Bible study pleasantly surprised at how much I learned, and I made plans to attend again. I could not believe the Bible was so interesting and *so relevant* to things that mattered to me. Bowling would have to wait next time.

After that meeting, I began looking at love differently. I read back through my notes, and I thought about the relationship I was in. I looked for the "ifs" and "becauses" between us. I thought a lot about 1 Corinthians 13, and I realized that the sort of love the Bible talked about was not what we had. I had a new understanding of love, and our relationship fell short, by a long shot.

Most of the ideas of love we see on TV or in movies are very different from what the Bible teaches about love. Love is often portrayed as a feeling that sweeps you off your feet and carries your relationship from the first eye-lock across the room till death do you part. This is really "love if" and "love because," conditional feelings without the commitment that true love requires.

The Bachelor and shows like it have been around for years. Although young women often say they just watch it for laughs, it has influenced how our culture views love and relationships. Have you noticed that almost all of the relationships formed on these shows end within a few months after the final rose is given? *The Bachelor* has a five percent success rate for couples staying together.[4] FIVE percent. There's a reason for this horribly low success rate. Shows like that are all about competition and chemistry. "Love if" and "love because" reign supreme, but ultimately no one wants love like that. They are cheap substitutes, and the truth comes out after the cameras are gone.

> Were you aware that the giddy, romantic feelings of love last on average two years?

When you know what true love is, it will help you recognize "love if" and "love because" and protect you from getting sucked into a fake love that is all feelings and no commitment. A lot of what is called love these days is really selfishness disguised.

Were you aware that the giddy, romantic feelings of love

that come when you first "fall in love" with someone only last on average *two* years?[5] That's it! These strong feelings that attract you to someone initially are actually designed to fade. This is very important information to know, because many couples are building their relationships based on these initial feelings of romantic attraction they have for each other. These feelings are very powerful and are very real, but they were not designed to last forever. They are not enough to sustain a lasting, enjoyable marriage by themselves. Those giddy initial feelings are designed to draw us into a relationship with a person, but the love that develops through mutual commitment and deeper knowledge of each other is necessary to grow and sustain a relationship long term. If you base love only on these romantic feelings, you are setting yourself up for future disappointment—two or so years later to be exact.

> *We both understood that love was more than just a feeling.*

When Sean and I dated, I could hardly sleep at night because I was such a mess in my feelings for him. It became even worse when we married. The way we looked at each other. The way we talked to each other. We were just plain goofy. We can't even watch videos from those early days. It's embarrassing! Hear me say this, those initial feelings of attraction that draw you into a relationship are good. Please don't marry someone who doesn't give you those "lovin' feelings," but I want to emphasize that true love is more than that.

Because Sean and I entered our dating relationship with the same ideas about what true love is, we didn't let the strong feelings we had for each other prompt us to say things we couldn't commit to yet. We chose not to use the word *love*. Instead, we used the word *like*, and we used it *a lot*. We both understood that love was more than just a feeling. For us, love was reserved only for marriage, because it represented the unconditional commitment we would one day make to our spouse to love each other regardless.

You might think that is odd, but don't you hate it when a guy tells you he loves you and then disappears later? *Exactly*. True love requires a commitment. Well, Sean waited until he could make that commitment before professing his love. He didn't mess with my heart, and I appreciate that. The first time he told me that he loved me was right before he asked me to marry him, and he's been loving me ever since.

If you enter marriage with "love if" or "love because," what happens when the feelings wear off and you can't keep up with the expectations? Will he leave you? Will you leave him?

Every now and then the fun rush of emotions comes back when Sean walks in the room, just like it did in the early days. It is nice when they come visit, but our marriage is based on more than those fickle feelings. When they leave, we do not panic. Our love is steady and strong. If you don't know about the fading aspect of the romantic feelings, you'll panic when they begin to fade. You may think, *Oh no, did I marry the wrong guy?* I think many married couples miss out on the wonderfulness of "love regardless" because they weren't prepared for how true love works.

In the midst of the realities of our marriage—paying bills, handling responsibilities at work, raising kids, managing the house, working through differences, and resolving conflicts—the tingly, romantic feelings come and go, but our love is steady as we learn to place each other's needs before our own. It is not always sexy to fold socks or romantic to work through an argument, but it is true love.

In twenty years of marriage, Sean has never taken me out in a canoe on a sun-twinkled lake surrounded by swans, like actors do in the movies. However, he has handed me all of the month's "fun money" when our budget was tight so I could go out and buy something new, saving none of it for himself. Twinkly lakes and swans aren't real. Tight budgets and sacrificial love however are *very* real. I would not trade love like this for anything.

So, that's how I learned about true love. Love was all God's idea, and He knows how it works best. We learn about true love in the Bible, because Jesus Himself loves us with the "love regardless" kind of love. When we experience His love, we are able to give that kind of love to others.

It's also how the Bible won me over. I keep finding great stuff in the Bible that continues to help me in my daily life. It isn't irrelevant at all like I originally thought. Now, looking back after twenty years of an enjoyable marriage, the Bible has been and still is a trusted source of information for me about love and relationships. I highly recommend it. In fact, my Bible is now worn around the edges and held together with some duct tape.

You can love your husband, before you even have one, by finding out about true love.

Key Truth
We love each other because he loved us first. 1 John 4:19

Points to Ponder
What kind of love are you hoping to find?

Action Step

Write out 1 Corinthians 13:4–7. Use this definition of love to evaluate yourself and your relationships. Try to memorize as much of it as you can, so you'll be able to recognize true love from fake love the next time a guy whispers that he loves you.

Endnotes

1. 1 Corinthians 13:4–7.

2. 1 John 4:8.

3. John 15:12.

4. Melissa Davidson, "So How Many of the Bachelor Couples Are Actually Still Together," Rise: News, http://risenews.net/2016/09/so-how-many-of-the-bachelor-couples-are-actually-still-together/ (Note: Ben and Lauren broke up after this post).

5. Gary Chapman, *Things I Wish I'd Known Before We Got Married* (Chicago: Northfield Publishing, 2010), 18.

For a long time I beat myself up about what I had done in the past with guys and also continued to get more and more bitter toward those guys as the years went on. When I understood the gospel and the forgiveness that Christ gives, I realized I had been forgiven when I deserved it the least, so I could forgive even when others didn't deserve it. Understanding true forgiveness in Christ freed me from a lot of past hurt that had been rooted in me for years and years.

—**Catherine, twenty-five years old**

I'll never forget the day I had to sit in front of Will, my virgin, soon-to-be husband, and tell him I had not saved myself for him. In fact, I had been impure with multiple different guys and physically there was nothing I could offer him that I had not already given to someone else. However, God used this moment to be the most tangible form of forgiveness I have ever experienced outside of my salvation. Will, like Christ, looked me in the eye and said, "There is nothing you've done that God's forgiveness doesn't cover. His grace is sufficient for you. I love you, and I FORGIVE YOU."
I am convinced that forgiving others is one of the most powerful things we can do as followers of Christ. Every day Will and I give and embrace forgiveness, because without it, we wouldn't be married.

—**Gracen, twenty-four, married two years**

2

Deleted Scenes

Experience Real Forgiveness

Behind the scenes of college life, I wrestled with the fact that I was not who I wanted to be. Guilt hovered over me and wouldn't go away. I regretted some decisions I had made and cringed about some things I had done. I kept trying to do good things to make myself feel better. I made a point to be really nice to everyone. I gave people rides when they asked. I even visited veterans in the hospital. None of it was working—not even a little bit. Regret has a relentless way of gnawing at your conscience, and it was gnawing me to death.

About that time I moved in with Kathy, the roommate I mentioned in the last chapter. She was joyful and loving, and there was something really different about her. Kathy was a very spiritual person. She actually enjoyed going to church and reading her Bible. She went to our sorority parties, but she didn't do all of the things the rest of us did.

I was a fairly private person back then, so I didn't talk openly about my inner struggles—especially stuff I was embarrassed about. I definitely didn't talk about religion either, but Kathy talked about her faith in God as easily as she talked about her classes or what she found shopping. After I had visited the Bible study with her a few times, a spiritual openness began to form between us.

One day I tiptoed into a spiritual conversation with her. "Kathy, I know you're a Christian. I think I am, but I'm not sure because you are really different from me." It didn't take long before I was crying and spilling my guts about the guilt I felt.

She pulled out a sheet of paper and said, "Kim, write down everything on here that you feel guilty for." After she assured me numerous times that she wouldn't read the list, I poured my little heart out onto that paper, emptying everything I could think of.

While I was doing that, she tore another sheet of paper to look like a cross. When I was finished, she asked me to fold up my list. After assuring me one more time that she wouldn't read it, I handed my list to her, and she pinned it to that paper cross.

As she held the paper cross with my list of sins attached, she shared with me that I felt guilty because I was guilty. God had a standard, and I fell short of it. Everybody, in fact, falls short. Then she started talking about Jesus. She said, "Kim, when Jesus died on the cross, He died for these sins. If you were the only person in the world, He would have still gone to the cross to die for you. He came back to life again, and if you will ask Him to forgive you of your sins, He will. He won't remember them anymore."

Could there be any better news to a heavy heart? She pulled out her Bible and showed me,

Though your sins are like scarlet, I will make them as white as snow. Though they are red like crimson, I will make them as white as wool.[1]

She also showed me:

I will remember their sins no more.[2]

Then she ripped up my guilty list.

As she tore the list up, my view of Jesus changed. He stepped off the dusty religious shelf in my mind, and He became real to me. Jesus actually cared about me. He took upon Himself the consequences of my mistakes so that I could be forgiven. I believed in that moment that He was who He said He was and that He could do what He said He could do, and something changed inside of me.

Later when I was alone, I prayed about all the things we had talked about. I thanked Jesus for dying in my place for my sin, and I asked Him to forgive me and make me the person He wanted me to be.

So that's my story of how I experienced real forgiveness and started my relationship with God.

I'm not a super emotional feely type person, but I remember walking across campus afterward and everything seemed so much brighter. The guilt and shame that had been weighing me down were gone. It felt good to be forgiven and to know that things were right between me and God.

What about you? Have you experienced God's forgiveness in your life?

You may be thinking, "Of course I'm not perfect, but I feel like I'm actually a pretty good person. I don't know if I really need forgiveness."

Although we may be able to look around and feel like a good person compared with others, the Bible says that we are not being measured by how we compare to other people, but by how we compare to God. Here's a run-through of the Ten Commandments, the first laws God really laid out for his people, to help you see how you stack up to God's standard of goodness.[3]

The Ten Commandments[4]

You must not have any other god but me.
Who's number one in your life? Would those around you say the same thing? During my life I've put a lot of people and things ahead of God. How about you?

You must not make for yourself an idol.
Perhaps you are picturing a little idol statue right now. You may say "I'm actually good on this one!" However, people often create in their head the type of god they want. They say stuff like, "Oh, MY god would never judge someone. He is only loving." But we can't just make God into who we want Him to be. That is called idolatry.

You must not misuse the name of the LORD your God.
God says His name is special. If the name of God is used as an exclamation or in profanity, His name is being misused. This has become so commonplace in our everyday language, music, movies, we hardly even notice.

Remember to observe the Sabbath day by keeping it holy.
I don't know about you, but I went to church maybe twice my freshman year.

Honor your father and mother.
Ever said anything bad about your parents?

You must not murder.
Most likely you haven't killed anyone. But the Bible also says if we hate someone, we've already committed murder in our hearts. That's a game changer for most of us.

You must not commit adultery.
Adultery is having sex with someone who isn't your husband. Jesus later added that looking at someone lustfully is also adultery.[5] Yikes! Let's just move on to the next one.

You must not steal.
Have you ever taken something that didn't belong to you, regardless of its value? Stealing answers on a test? Not paying for music or movies? Keeping the extra change even though you knew it wasn't rightfully yours?

You must not testify falsely against your neighbor.
Ever told a lie? Embellished a story? Spread a rumor?

You must not covet.
Have you ever wanted something someone else had? Their figure? Their clothes? Their boyfriend? Their life?

So how did you do? 3 out of 10? 8 out of 10? The Bible actually tells us that "we all fall short of God's glorious standard."[6] No one can look at that list and say they've never done any of them. I know I can't.

Let's say hypothetically that I did just one of these each day while I was in college. That wasn't too bad, was it?

One sin a day for four years actually adds up to 1,460 offenses. God is holy, and sin is a big deal. Jesus never sinned—not even once.[7] The Bible says it takes only one sin to separate me from God.[8] Having 1,460 offenses on my record isn't going to cut it.

Let's be honest, we all need it.

I am grateful for God's forgiveness. Let's be honest, we all need it. I'm thankful He gives it so generously when we ask for it.

And because I have graciously experienced forgiveness when I didn't deserve it, I know I must turn around and offer that kind of forgiveness to others when I am wronged. I have yet to have to forgive someone 1,460 times. All of my relationships, especially my marriage, are better because I have received the gift of forgiveness.

When relational conflicts come, remembering I was forgiven for wrongs against *God* helps me let go of wrongs done to *me*.

A marriage is made up of two selfish people, who are different from each other, who are learning to love and care for one another and function as a team. If you are doing life alongside someone who is different from you (and trust me, any male you marry will be different from you), you will experience conflict. If you want to have a great marriage someday, you need to be equipped to deal with the conflict that will come. There will be times when you'll be wronged. Sometimes it will be your husband's fault, and it will hurt. But if you have spent time before marriage learning to forgive, you will be better able to extend forgiveness to your spouse. If you want to love your husband, before you even have one, you'll need to learn how to forgive.

Listen to what "America's marriage therapist" Gary Chapman says,

There are no healthy marriages
without sincere apologies and genuine forgiveness.
If you learn how to apologize and forgive,
you have in place two of the major elements
for building a successful marriage.[9]

Forgiveness Pop Quiz

True False   1. Forgiveness is something you feel.
True False   2. Forgiveness is forgetting.
True False   3. Forgiveness means that you let a person continue to hurt you.
True False   4. Forgiveness involves getting someone back for hurting you.
True False   5. Forgiveness means all consequences of the offense are taken away.

(1. False. It's a choice. 2. False, It's a choice. 3. False 4. False 5. False)[10]

So what does forgiveness look like?

Forgiveness is the choice to live with the consequences
of someone else's sin without getting bitter.

This may sound difficult to do, and it is. No one wants to deal with someone else's consequences. But forgiveness is essential for your emotional health and the health of your relationships.

If you want to be emotionally healthy,
you will need to experience forgiveness personally.

If you want good relationships,
you will need to be able to forgive others.

Maybe you are thinking of a situation in which that seems impossible. The wonderful thing is that experiencing God's forgiveness when we don't deserve it increases our ability to forgive others when they don't deserve it.

Forgive as the Lord forgave you.[11]

Sean and I strive to keep short accounts with each other. This just means that we deal with issues as they come. We have found that if you let issues build up, it gets harder to deal with them later.

It seems as if we are asking for forgiveness from each other pretty often. Let's see, last Friday I said something that made Sean feel unimportant. He had opened up and shared a frustration he was having in life, and I later made a comment that came across flippantly, like I had disregarded his feelings. I hurt him. I had to ask for forgiveness.

Sean was grumpy and withdrawn for a few days this week. He knew he had probably caused some hurt with his attitude. The boys and I were grateful when he came back and apologized to us later.

Giving and receiving forgiveness is just a part of life in our home, and it all began years ago when I first experienced real forgiveness.

You can love your husband, before you even have one, by experiencing real forgiveness, so that you will be able to forgive.

Key Truth
Make allowance for each other's faults, and forgive anyone who offends you. Remember, the Lord forgave you, so you must forgive others. Colossians 3:13

Points to Ponder
Have you really experienced God's forgiveness in your life?

Action Step
Go through the Ten Commandments list again and write out all the things you need forgiveness for on a sheet of paper. Get things right with God. As in my situation, it might be beneficial to talk through it with a Christian you can trust.

Endnotes
1. Isaiah 1:18.
2. Hebrews 8:12b (ESV).
3. Shout out to Ray Comfort for his insight on this. Ray Comfort, *Hell's Best Kept Secret* (Springdale, PA:Whitaker House,1989).
4. Exodus 20:3–17.
5. Matthew 5:27–28.
6. Romans 3:23.
7. Hebrews 4:15.
8. James 2:10.
9. Gary Chapman, *What I Wish I'd Known Before We Got Married* (Chicago: Northfield Publishing, 2010), p.72.
10. These insights were taken from the chapter on forgiveness in *Victory Over the Darkness*. Neil T. Anderson, *Victory Over the Darkness: Realizing the Power of Your Identity in Christ* (Ventura, CA: Regal Books, 2000), chapter 11.
11. Colossians 3:13 (NIV).

I never thought I would be strong enough to end a three-year relationship. I was willing to give God everything else, but this part terrified me. An unhealthy, high school relationship had been the most steady thing in my life over the past few years, and I had a hard time believing that God's best for me was to take away what I thought was keeping me steady. Turns out, God's best for me was better than I could have ever imagined. To this day I am thankful that I chose to put God first in every area of my life, specifically dating relationships.
—**Ashley, twenty years old**

Making God my priority was the best decision I have ever made! It helped me to know who He was. And in return, I was able to know who I was! My second best decision was marrying my husband. But if God wasn't my priority then I would never have known where to start.
—**Megan, thirty-one, married three months**

After forty-six years of marriage I want to take this opportunity to share that God has been faithful to make marriage more than I could have ever asked. It would have something to do with the fact that it takes three to make two equal one. Two wills meshing is impossible without the Spirit of God, but as both take their surrendered hearts to Him, He brings true unity in a deeper way than mere humans can imagine.
—**Brenda, married forty-six years**

3

Core Exercise

Put God First

Experiencing God's forgiveness was changing things for me. Where there was once regret, there was now hope and peace. God had done this for me, and I wanted to know more about Him. I was ready to do life His way, and that meant some things were going to be different.

"I want to start following God."

Hunched over my landline phone, I timidly whispered these words to my fiancé. It was late, and my roommate was already asleep. I didn't want to wake her, so I pulled the phone out into the hallway of my sorority floor to talk. Every now and then, a girl would step around me on her way to the bathroom. Explaining my new relationship with God to my fiancé was not going well.

I wanted him to want a relationship with God too, but it wasn't happening as I hoped. He was having a difficult time understanding where I was coming from and why I wanted to change. I tried to answer his questions. I wasn't doing a great job explaining everything, but I knew that I didn't want to go back to a life that wasn't centered on God.

We were not making much progress.

After I got off the phone and laid my head on my pillow, I couldn't shake the thought: *What if I lose him over this?* I really believed he was the one for me. We were engaged to be married. I knew I could no longer do life without God, but would I be able to do life without my fiancé?

A few weeks later, I would find out.

After giving him multiple opportunities to pursue God alongside me, he continued to be resistant. At one point he just rolled his eyes and said, "C'mon, Kim, don't get all religious on me." I wasn't sure what to do. I wanted to start living my life the way God wanted, but I was engaged to someone who didn't want that. Was I supposed to stay with him since we were already engaged?

I turned to my roommate, Kathy, who had introduced me to Christ: "What should I do?" She called the campus pastor at her church and put me on the phone with him. I cried the whole time. He suggested I read through some verses on relationships.

Equipped with the list of verses he had recommended (see page 54), I drove home to my parents' house for the weekend. I found two Bibles on our bookshelf. I had never really done anything like this before, so I was thankful one of the Bibles was in a version that was easy to understand. I sat down at our dining room table, opened the Bibles, and looked up all those verses by myself. I can only imagine what my parents were thinking.

I had to figure this out. What did the Bible say about marriage? What did it say about dating? What did it say about sex? Was there anything in it that said I needed to stay with him since we were already engaged?

The Bible was no longer irrelevant to me. I came across this verse in my study:

Do not be unequally yoked together with unbelievers.[1]

I wondered what "yoked" meant and discovered it was "joined together."[2] I realized that marriage would join our lives together. I was now a believer. I couldn't figure out how to put God first in my life when my fiancé was so opposed to it. I had given him many opportunities to learn about God too, but he resisted them. My fiancé was at a place where he didn't want any changes in his life, in my life, or in our relationship. The Bible said that I should not be tied together with an unbeliever, and we were not married yet.

It was scary, but my decision was made. I closed both of the Bibles, hugged my parents, and headed back to college. I picked my fiancé up that night, and we drove to the park on campus. As I shared in the opening chapter, sitting in my car that night, I broke off our engagement.

Oh yeah, I forgot to mention one *tiny, little* important detail. My fiancé and I were not only engaged, we were also anatomy lab partners. The two of us were dissecting a cat together. *Could this be any worse? How in the world were we going to finish out the semester?* It was too late to drop the class.

Kathy scribbled out a Bible verse for me on an index card, and I carried it with me as I began the long walk across campus to lab. I said that verse over and over to myself: *For I can do everything through Christ, who gives me strength.*[3] By the time I made it to class, I had memorized my first Bible verse! I couldn't believe how helpful memorizing a Bible verse was. I was also quite relieved when he didn't show up.

The days that followed the breakup felt uncertain and awkward, but I made it through the first day and the next and the next. Each day became a little easier. He eventually showed up for lab. We made it through, but things would never be the same between us.

There were mixed reactions from my friends. Some thought I was crazy to break up with him because of my relationship with God. Some said I wasn't being patient enough. Others encouraged me that it was a good decision.

Was I completely crazy? Was I throwing my life away because of "religion"?

It was too late at that point to change my decision, and I would have to face the results of it. As I lay in bed at night, I wondered what my future life would be like. *Would God take care of me? Would I ever get married?*

Thirty years later, how do I look back on my decision to put God first? With absolute gratitude.

I wish I could go back in time and whisper in my ear, "You're making the right decision. I know it is hard, but following God is worth it, no matter the cost."

Making the decision to put God first might have been scary back then, but it was one of the best decisions I ever made in my life. It wasn't easy, and others didn't understand, but I am so thankful I made the choice to put God first even when it cost me what I treasured most at the time. Even if I hadn't found Sean years later, following God's plan would still have been worth it, no matter what.

That one decision put me on a track to experience God's very best. He knows how life and relationships should work. His instructions and commands in the Bible are not meant to cheat us out of life. God tells us what to do and not do because He loves us and cares for us. His commands protect us and provide the very best for us.

Basically, there are three different ways we can respond to God. These responses are represented below by three circles.

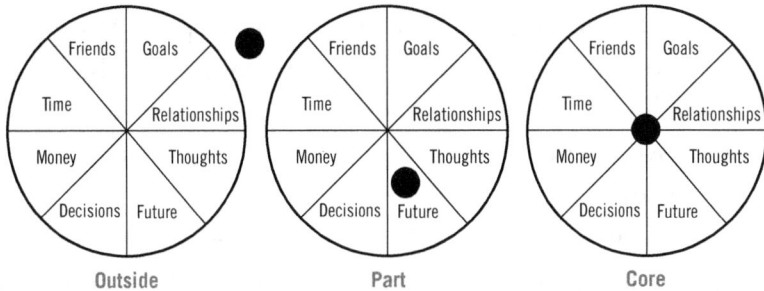

do and not do because He loves us and cares for us. His commands protect us and provide the very best for us.

The first circle represents those with God outside of their lives. Either they just don't know what God wants or they don't care, but they live without God in their lives.

The second circle represents those who have God in their lives, but only as a part. They might go to church and even read their Bible, but when push comes to shove, God only influences a small part of their lives. Because they limit the areas God influences, this person can sometimes look the same as the person without God in their life.

The third circle represents those with God in the center or "core" of their lives. He not only is in their life, but He touches every part of it. This person wants to know what God says, and then tries to live life in obedience to Him in every area.

If you want to be the "core" circle, but you tie yourself to someone living in one of the other circles, you will always have inner or outer tension. You will feel inner conflict deciding between doing what God wants and what will please the person you are with, or your relationship will have tension because you disagree at such a fundamental level. It will be difficult for you to do what God wants if you are tied to someone who doesn't want to follow God — that's why the Bible warns about being "unequally yoked." Something will have to give.

I have found many young women will sacrifice what they really believe is best for the sake of keeping their man. Many hope that they will be able to change him, but over time, guys in these other circles change them instead. I have rarely seen a young woman authentically bring a guy to the third circle.

If you want to increase your odds for a God-centered marriage for the long haul, you need to live a God-centered life on your own for a while, apart from a guy. Then, because people usually end up marrying someone they date, you should only date a man who has been living that way too.

Marriage ties you together in every way imaginable.

Evidence of a track record is important, because sometimes a guy may pretend to be more committed to a relationship with God than he actually is in order to please a girl he is dating or wanting to date. In fact, I just heard a story this week of a young girl whose boyfriend, whom she thought was interested in God, completely reverted back to living without God after they broke up. If you want a God-centered marriage, it's important to meet a guy who has already demonstrated living with God in the center of his life *before* you start a relationship with him.

When Sean came along, I had been living in the third circle for years. He had been living that way too. When we started dating, we had both independently established having God and His Word as a priority in our lives. Since

Sean and I are equally yoked together, we don't pull against each other and experience the tension that comes with that. We are a team, keeping God in the center, and we are able to spur one another on along the way.

Marriage ties you together in every way imaginable. As a married couple, you will be making numerous decisions together—more than I ever realized as single woman.

Some decisions are small, but some have big ramifications. For example, years ago Sean and I were faced with a decision about reporting some extra income. We chose to be honest and not leave out any information. Turning in this income ended up costing us thousands of dollars in taxes. If we had lied about it, it wouldn't have cost us so much financially. But because we were both living in the third circle, our relationship with God touched every area of our lives, including our finances and our character. We chose to be honest, even though it cost us a considerable amount of money.

If we had been in two different circles, this decision could have caused tension in our relationship. Instead, it actually brought us closer together as we trusted God in the midst of it. Even though Sean and I are very different people, with different personalities, we both try very hard to line up with what God says in every area of our lives. As different as we are, putting God first connects us at the deepest level. When push comes to shove, it matters more to both of us what God thinks over what we individually think. We decided to do what we felt God would want us to do, and then we had to trust Him to take care of us, which He did.

I can't imagine facing a decision like that if we had been in different circles, and this is only one tough decision of many we have had to make in our marriage. Marrying someone in the same circle as you doesn't just impact where and how often you go to church. Whether or not you and your future husband both want to put God first in your family will affect the direction your family will go and decisions you will make every day.

As the picture below illustrates, as you put God first and grow closer to God, and as your husband puts God first and grows closer to God, you will experience not only a deeper closeness with God, but with your husband also.

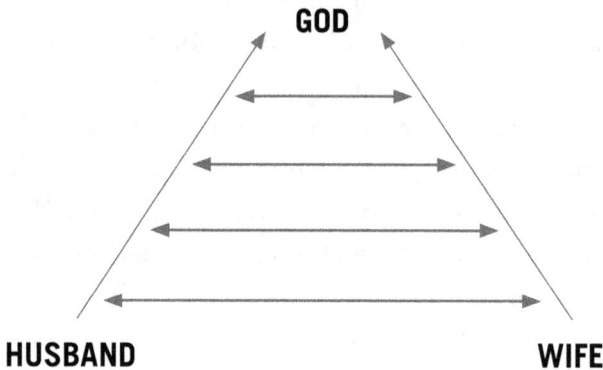

GOD

HUSBAND   **WIFE**

**You can love your husband,
before you even have one,
by choosing to put God first in your life.**

**By choosing a man who has also chosen to put
God first in his life, you can work as a team to
form a God-centered family.**

Key Truth:
Seek the Kingdom of God above all else, and live righteously, and he will give you everything you need. Matthew 6:33

Points to Ponder
Is there a person or a habit that is keeping you from putting God first?

Action Step
Ask a friend "Which circle would you say best represents my life?"

Resource
My Heart—Christ's Home, by Robert Boyd Munger (Inter-Varsity Press) This little booklet has helped encourage me to put God first.

Endnotes
1. 2 Corinthians 6:14a (NKJV).
2. *Webster's New World Pocket Dictionary*, s.v. "yoked."
3. Philippians 4:13.

Dating and Marriage Verses and Questions

Genesis 1;2	*Matthew 6:33–34*
2 Samuel 11;12	*Romans 12:12–14*
Job 31:1–12	*1 Corinthians 7*
Proverbs 10:19	*1 Corinthians 11:7–12*
Proverbs 12:4, 22	*1 Corinthians 13*
Proverbs 15:1	*2 Corinthians 6:14–18*
Proverbs 16:24	*Ephesians 4:32*
Proverbs 19:11, 14	*Ephesians 5:18–33*
Proverbs 18:22	*1 Thessalonians 4:1–8*
Proverbs 21:9, 19	*1 Timothy 5:2*
Proverbs 27:15-17	*2 Timothy 2:20–22*
Proverbs 29:5	*Hebrews 13:4*
Proverbs 31:10–31	*1 Peter 3:1–7*

1. Is dating scriptural?
2. What is the purpose of dating?
3. What should be my motivations for dating?
4. Contrast love vs. infatuation.
5. Should a Christian date a non-Christian?
6. Name the positive benefits of dating? Dangers and pitfalls?
7. What should my standards be concerning the physical aspect of dating?
8. Do the standards change as the relationship progresses?
9. What is the purpose of marriage?
10. How will I know who to marry?
11. How will I know the right time to marry?
12. What is the purpose of the engagement period?
13. List the qualities, characteristics, goals, and interests of the person I'd like to marry.
14. Should I have expectations?
15. What is the husband's role in marriage?
16. What is the wife's role?
17. Standards for me in dating, based on scriptural principles and standards:
    a. What type of person will I date?
    b. How often to date and how much?
    c. What attitude will I have toward the person I am dating?
    d. How will I treat that person?
    e. What will I talk about and do on dates?
    f. Where is dating on my priority list?
    g. How will my relationship with God affect my dating and how will my dating relationship affect my fellowship with God?

Although my college years have been some of my absolute favorites, they have also been some of the hardest. Whether it was tough family situations or my own battle with depression and anxiety, it felt like every season was a season of change and a new season of difficulty. It would have been easy to define myself and my worth by current circumstances; however, I'm thankful that throughout my college years I learned to believe what God says about how valuable I really am.

—**Shelby, twenty-one years old**

———————

I'm married to an extremely godly man who showers me with affection, but when I try to find all my value in his affirming words it can leave me feeling like I need more. The days when I can confidently believe my value comes from God are when my husband's words of affirmation mean so much more. I've learned that I can never fully be satisfied with finding my value in my husband's words because God made me to only find value in Him.

—**Kelsey, twenty-six, married two years**

4

Always a Bridesmaid

Believe Your Value

"Kim, I'm getting married! Would you be my bridesmaid?"

I had this honor not once, or twice, not three times, or four, or six, or eight, not ten, nor twelve times. As a single girl, I was a bridesmaid in thirteen weddings. Thirteen.

If you also count reading Scripture, serving cake, cleaning up afterward, or assisting brides with various other tasks, the number of weddings I was a part of climbs even higher.

Fortunately, I was never asked to sing.

In all honesty, I was *truly happy* for my close friends and family members who were getting married, and I was *incredibly honored* to be a part of their special day. But, I have to admit, every time someone close to me was chosen, it was a stinging reminder that I hadn't been.

When my beautiful younger sister got married before me, most assumed that since I wasn't married, I was the younger sister. *No, I'm the older, unmarried sister. Thanks.*

Then my handsome younger brother got married. The same assumptions were made at his wedding. *No, I'm the oldest, still unmarried sister. Sigh.*

Then my dad got remarried *before* I got married. Sometimes you just have to own it and laugh.

Not only did I become a professional bridesmaid with some mad wedding cake serving skills, but I also became a dominant force at catching bridal bouquets. I lost track of how many I caught, but as a six-foot-one woman with a wide wingspan, my petite co-bridesmaids never had a chance. *Might as well make the most of it, you know?*

My self-worth was in detox.

It should be noted that out of all the weddings I either attended or was a bridesmaid in, I had a date only *once*. Well maybe twice, if you count Jack from Texas.[1] He was one of those undefined, confusing, ongoing "friendships" I found myself in. *We rode to a wedding together in the same car, so that's basically a date. Right?*

For a girl who once found most of her value and confidence in having a guy, singleness was a tough season for me.

As I told you in the last chapter, I was engaged to another guy earlier in life, and that relationship provided a steady dose of attention. He made me feel pretty and desirable, so I felt good about myself. After our engagement ended, I felt a bit lost. I guess I didn't realize how much I based my value in having him until he was gone.

My self-worth was in detox. Going cold turkey without a guy was rough. There were times that I just wanted to go find another guy to get some attention, but as a new follower of Christ, I had decided to do relationships differently. Deep down I didn't really want to chase a guy or use someone just to make myself feel better, but it was tempting. At times I thought about going back to some of my old habits and outfits to get a guy to notice me, but doing those things just didn't feel right anymore.

I needed a new way to feel good about myself, so I chose a new hairstyle. I got a perm.

Well, my perm expectations were a little too high, and it didn't transform my life as I had hoped. As all of my friends were falling in love around me, and I was the dateless bridesmaid with a perm gone wrong, I began to wonder:

Would I ever be in a relationship again? Would I ever feel noticed or pretty?

One day I was reading Psalm 139 in the Bible. As I read the words, it struck me for the first time that God was speaking about *me*! Seeing that God viewed me in such an intimate, tender way made me feel special.

Excerpts from Psalm 139

You know when I sit down or stand up.
Really? Who takes the time to notice something as insignificant as that? He keeps track of whether I am sitting or standing?

You see me when I travel and when I rest at home.
You know everything I do.
You know how when you like a guy and are always aware of where he is? That's the way the God of the Universe is with me—and you.

You know what I am going to say even before I say it.
I don't know what goes through your thoughts, but I'm amazed He knows my thoughts yet still wants a relationship with me.

I can never escape from your Spirit!
I can never get away from your presence!
Wherever I go, I can never get away from His presence in my life.
Despite where I have been, He still wants a relationship with me.
Unbelievable.

Even in darkness I cannot hide from you.
I couldn't hide from Him, even if I tried, and this is strangely comforting
to me.

You made me so wonderfully complex!
If He formed me and made me just the way He wanted to, then maybe
there wasn't anything wrong with me after all.

You watched me as I was being formed in utter seclusion, as
I was woven together in the dark of the womb.
Whoa. Really? He was there with me?

You saw me before I was born.
Every day of my life was recorded in your book.
Every moment was laid out before a single day had passed.
He saw me before anyone else? He scheduled each day of my life before
I began to breathe? Perhaps He really was in control of all my life's
events, and there was a purpose behind everything.

How precious are your thoughts about me, O God.
They cannot be numbered!
He thinks of me that much? So much that I can't even count the number
of times?

And when I wake up, you are still with me!
When I wake up, He's thinking about me? The Creator of the universe is
thinking about ME as I wake up each day?

How in the world is He able to do this for so many
people? I have no idea. I mean, who am I that He would
even care? I have since learned from the Bible that my
value to God doesn't come from anything I can do or
produce. I am valuable to Him because He created me for
a relationship with Him. He even sacrificed His Son, Jesus,

to make a relationship with me possible. Because I can't do anything to earn His love, I also can't do anything to lose it. I may never be able to wrap my mind around it, but I am just going to enjoy that I am so special to Him.

Psalm 139 meant so much to me that I decided to memorize it so I could think about it often. I copied the passage out of my Bible and taped it to my bathroom mirror.

Each morning when I was getting ready, I would memorize a few more words.

I began to believe that, even though I couldn't see God, He was very active and involved in my life. If God valued me enough to notice when I sat down or stood up, then maybe I was pretty valuable — even if a guy wasn't interested in me. I began to feel special because of what God thought of me. As I thought about how God viewed me, it started slowly changing how I viewed myself.

Little did I realize it at the time, but this new discovery of finding my worth and value in how God viewed me was one of the best things that could have happened to me and my future marriage.

I know now if I had gone into marriage finding my security in my looks or in my man, I would have set my marriage up for problems. Here's why:

Beauty doesn't last

The Bible is right: "beauty does not last."[2] If you have a lot of money and really good genes, you might be able to postpone the signs of aging a little. Even with high-dollar creams, Botox, and plastic surgery, there's still no way to completely avoid wrinkles, cellulite, gray hairs, and stretch marks. Even the most beautiful women cannot escape getting older. If you place your value in how you look, then what will you do later when your looks fade? Remember, our goal here is a *lasting* marriage. You know, long-term, old age. You are in your peak years in your twenties and thirties, and I hate to break the news to you, but things will start going downhill after that. Literally. If I find my value in how I look, what happens when my body sags, and I don't look like I once did? What happens when I put on forty pounds during pregnancy? What happens when someone prettier comes along? If we want to be truly secure, confident women, we need something more stable than our looks to base it on.

Your husband will not meet all your needs

If you place your value in what a man thinks of you, what will you do when you aren't getting the feels from him? Let's just admit it: we have a lot of needs. We want to be understood and loved and cared for and protected. We want to feel pretty and special. We want to be chosen, pursued, and cherished. These are valid needs.

Often we think these needs will be met in a relationship and ultimately satisfied by our husband. Again, I hate to be the one to break it to you, but your husband will not be able to meet all of your needs. Even the best of men cannot meet *all* of your needs *all* of the time. He won't always understand where you are coming from. Sometimes he'll say the wrong thing or unintentionally do the wrong thing. There are times even as a wife when you won't feel special or cherished or pretty.

Personally, I think we have these deep needs so they will ultimately drive us to God, because He is the only one who can perfectly meet them. If we are looking to our spouse to meet needs that only God really can, we are placing some hefty expectations on our husband. He will feel incompetent and manipulated, and your marriage will have problems.

Sean is an amazing husband, and I appreciate his efforts to make me feel pretty and desirable. His sole purpose in life and marriage, however, is not to make me feel good about myself. If I come in expecting that from him each day, I will be like a giant vacuum cleaner, sucking the life out of him and our relationship. And if he is looking to me as his main source of affirmation each day, we will drain each other pretty quickly.

Tim Keller, author of the *The Meaning of Marriage*, nails it with this illustration:

> *The picture of marriage given here [in Ephesians 5] is not of two needy people, unsure of their own value and purpose, finding their significance and meaning in one another's arms. If you add two vacuums to each other, you only get a bigger and stronger vacuum, a giant sucking…If we look to our spouses to fill up our tanks in a way that only God can do, we are demanding an impossibility.*[3]

It's important that we come into relationships and marriage as strong individuals who are confident in our value apart from another person. This puts us in a position to have something to add to strengthen our marriage, rather than looking for what we can take from it.

Finding your worth and value in what Christ thinks of you is such a relief, because in His eyes your value never changes. God is not fickle like people are, so what He thinks of me is steadfast and unchanging. If Sean notices my new haircut, that's awesome; but if he doesn't, I can still feel confident in the way that God sees me. Having Sean's attention is great, but it isn't vital to my well-being. It is also wonderful to know my value doesn't change based on my performance. When I have bad days or mess up, I am still just as valuable in God's eyes.

Know what's crazy about all this? Listen to what Sean said about me in his book, *Unsatisfied*:

> *[Kim] blossomed into a bold and confident woman.*
> *I'm so thankful for her confidence because*
> *it was one of the first things that attracted me to her. I*
> *saw that and thought, "I gotta marry that girl!"*[4]

I'm pretty sure God has a sense of humor, because it's laughable to think that the insecure, dateless bridesmaid with a bad perm would someday catch a man's eye with her confidence! Thank you, God, for helping me believe my value.

You can love your husband, before you even have one, by finding your value and security in how God views you.

In Christ, my value doesn't come from
what I do
or what I have
or how I look.
Rather, my value comes
from what He did,
what He gave,
and how He looks at me.

Key Truth
God paid a high price for you. 1 Corinthians 7:23a

Points to Ponder
What makes you feel confident about yourself?

Action Step
Memorize some verses from Psalm 139. Try to eventually get all of them committed to memory. I highly recommend this. Feel free to borrow my "taped to the bathroom mirror" method.

Additional Resource
Victory Over the Darkness, Neil T. Anderson
This book has been super helpful to me in finding my value and identity in Christ.

Endnotes:
1. Not his real name.
2. Proverbs 31:30.
3. Timothy Keller, *The Meaning of Marriage: Facing the Complexities of Commitment with the Wisdom of God* (New York: Dutton, 2011), 52.
4. Sean Vollendorf, *Unsatisfied: Finding the Life You Can't Stop Looking For* (Fayetteville, AR: CMM Press, 2016), 136.

I never realized how tiring attempting to look perfect was until I learned that looking perfect wouldn't even bring me true joy. After hearing that my true beauty came from what was inside of me, rather than what was on the outside, I began to experience a peace and a joy I hadn't before. Knowing that a man appreciates what is on the inside is so refreshing, and knowing that God appreciates what is on the inside is so comforting.
—**Madison, twenty-one years old**

———————

Before I learned about the importance of modesty, I always wore clothing to emphasize certain parts of my body. I thought by doing this, it would up my chances of catching a guy's attention. When I realized the type of attention I was attracting was not from men of character, it changed my perspective on what I am telling the world with what I wear.
—**Christen, twenty-two years old**

———————

*You will attract a guy at the same spiritual and emotional maturity level as yourself.
So instead of waiting or looking for a husband, start preparing yourself now to become the kind of person your ideal husband would be attracted to.*
—**Wife, married eleven years**

5

Beyond Botox

Develop Inner Beauty

I was on my way to a campus meeting, and one of my friends asked if he could ride with me. We enjoyed a brief visit on the way, and before we got out of the car to go inside, my burly, masculine friend paused awkwardly and said, "Hey Kim, um, thanks for dressing modestly. I've noticed that about you, and I appreciate it. You know, you really model purity." He grinned, "You're pure like Ivory soap."[1] I smiled and thanked him. He had no idea how much that meant to me. It was a compliment I never expected to hear, and I graciously received it. I didn't know that being compared to soap would be so encouraging, but it was.

My inner self was getting a remodel, and I was glad that I was making progress. I had spent most of my life focused mainly on my outward appearance, but I was learning as I followed God that He cared more about what I was like on the inside, so I was trying to focus on that part of my life as well. On this particular day, I was given a refreshing reminder that God wasn't the only one who valued it. There were sharp young men out there who did too.

This inner self I'm referring to is often called character. It's the way you think, feel, and behave.[2] Character is who you are when no one else is looking, not just the part you want others to see. It's the REAL you. It's who you are when you're PMSing, swamped with homework, and your roommate is driving you nuts. When the real you comes out, is it attractive and appealing to others around you? It should be. That's what inner beauty is.

The Bible, of course, speaks on this.

Don't be concerned about the outward beauty of fancy hairstyles, expensive jewelry, or beautiful clothes. You should clothe yourselves instead with the beauty that comes from within, the unfading beauty of a gentle and quiet spirit, which is so precious to God.[3]

After reading that verse, some of you may be wondering if I wear makeup and fix my hair. Rest assured, I do. I color my gray hair, cover the dark circles under my eyes, and I'm a fan of Stitch Fix.[4] I do what I can to look my best, and Sean really appreciates that.

In my study Bible the verse reads,

Your adornment must not be merely external.[5]

Bible study pays off! The Bible doesn't forbid all "adornment," but the godly woman knows that it shouldn't be her main focus. These outer adornments—hairstyle, jewelry, and clothes—are not the source of her true beauty.

She is to be known for a beauty that comes from within, not the kind of beauty you can pick up at the mall.

One reason it is important to invest in your inner beauty while you are single is that it attracts men of character. Like attracts like. Men of character are attracted to women of character. If you want a man who has excellent character, then you need to be a woman of excellent character.

If you want to marry a king,
then you need to be a queen.[6]

There are lots of character qualities we could discuss here, but let's take dressing modestly, for example. Young women new to following God tend to resist dressing modestly. However, a man of excellent character is fighting for purity in his thoughts, and he might need to avoid a woman who makes that fight harder by what she is wearing. As my friend demonstrated in my opening story, he'll notice whether a woman dresses modestly. So, dressing modestly will actually attract the right kind of guy and repel the wrong ones. If you are dressing to impress, be sure you are impressing the right ones.

Here's another reason it's important to learn about inner beauty and develop it before you are married:

You can fake it with your date,
but you can't fake it with your mate.

Marriage will expose your true character like nothing else. (Well, besides raising kids, but our focus here is on marriage, so we will stay on topic.) After years of singleness and spiritual growth, I went into marriage feeling pretty good about my character. Boy was I surprised at how much growing I still had to do! There have been times in our marriage when Sean has seen

Inner beauty is within reach for all of us.

some of my less-than-beautiful character, and I have just wanted to run and hide. But you can't run and hide in marriage. He's going to see the real deal you. You're going to see the real deal him. I'm actually too embarrassed to share a personal example here, so we'll move on.

If, like most people, you are feeling you have a lot of room for improvement in this area, don't be too discouraged. The importance of inner beauty should actually encourage us, because the good thing about character is it can change. There are lots of things about ourselves we can't change—our body shape, aspects of our personality, our background, or the family we came from. But we *can change* our character! Inner beauty is within reach for all of us.

The Bible has a lot to say about character. It actually indicates that character comes in bundles. Things are sometimes sold in bundles, which means they come together as a collection, and you don't get to pick the items individually. I can't just pick a few from one bundle and a few from another. They come together as a group, which is good or bad, depending on which bundle you pick.

Here's Character Bundle A:
The Holy Spirit produces this kind of fruit in our lives: love, joy, peace, patience, kindness, goodness, faithfulness, gentleness, and self-control.[7]

Here's Character Bundle B:
When you follow the desires of your sinful nature, the results are very clear: sexual immorality, impurity,

lustful pleasures, … hostility, quarreling, jealousy,
outbursts of anger, selfish ambition, … division, … envy,
drunkenness, wild parties, and other sins like these.[8]

Which bundle best describes your life?

Option B may come more naturally to us, but if you have one from this list, the others may soon follow. Do we really want those qualities in our lives and relationships — hostility, quarreling, anger? If inner beauty is our goal, we'd better go after Bundle A. It's way more attractive. However, Bundle A requires letting God be in control of our lives.

Character is shaped by the level of God's control in our lives, but we also have an important role in developing our character. The Bible teaches you are to train yourself to be godly.[9] Just like working out, it is something that we can place effort into so we can get better.

Here are some examples of character qualities I've found absolutely essential in marriage. Be assured, I am still training in these areas too!

Gentle and Quiet Spirit

You should clothe yourselves instead with the beauty
that comes from within, the unfading beauty of a gentle
and quiet spirit, which is so precious to God.[10]

Often a girl will assume this means she needs a gentle and quiet personality. I'm the introverted quieter type, but some of my favorite godly women live out loud. I think a gentle and quiet spirit is possible for any personality.

Gentleness means, "I am going to accept all of God's dealings with me without retaliation, …knowing that God will work it out in my life."[11] It comes from trusting God's goodness and resting in His control. Some people panic in difficult situations and resort to "clutching" or "grabbing" what they think they need.[12] A gentle woman is not like that.

A quiet spirit is someone who is at rest on the inside. Because she trusts God, she can be at peace. She isn't out there clamoring for what she doesn't have. A girl can be super outgoing and be at rest on the inside. The opposite is also true. A girl can be quiet on the outside but in turmoil on the inside.

When life gets crazy and feels out of control, do we start grabbing for control, or can we rest in the knowledge that God is in control?

Kindness

Kindness is essential in a happy marriage. I had no idea this quality would be so critical. But in day-to-day life, it's simple kindnesses like "thank you" and "please" that can make or break a marriage. *Who knew?*

Normally when someone thinks of kindness they think of being really sweet or nice. Kindness can be those things, but my working definition of kindness is treating someone better than they deserve to be treated. God treats us kindly, and we are to be kind to those around us.[13]

When someone walks in the room grumpy and says something bristly, do we bristle back, or can we respond with a kinder word? Do we make the effort to appreciate the little things others do for us by saying "thank you" and "please"?

Contentment

When I was single, I once went on a walk with a married friend. She was processing through the fact that she wasn't able to have kids. I, of course, was processing through the fact that I didn't have a husband. We both wanted something we didn't have, and we found a connection between us as a result. I was so blown away that even though she had an incredible husband, she still longed for kids. I kept thinking, *Man, if I had a husband, I would never want or need anything else.* Of course, my own words haunted me after Sean and I got married and had trouble having kids.

Contentment is being happy with what you have. It's a wonderful quality. Many people go through life waiting for that next thing so *then* they can be happy. The ironic thing is, if you aren't able to be content in your current situation, then odds are you won't be content in your next situation either. If you aren't content single, then you probably won't be content being married.

There are good and hard things about both. Contentment is the ability to be thankful for the good in all things.

Are you able to be happy with what you have, or are you always wanting something else?

The good news about becoming a woman of godly character is that it makes you more beautiful. In a world that is so consumed with beauty, it's tough to keep up. Age can diminish our physical beauty, but have you ever known a godly woman who just seemed to grow more beautiful with age? The benefit of more birthdays is more time to grow in our character. Inner beauty is attractive, and a woman of character will shine brighter than others.

Most summers our family would spend six weeks in Florida at a program for college students. It's pretty awesome to be in a beach town, but I was continually surrounded by youth and beauty. As I sat by the kiddie pool one day with my three sons, young tan girls with cute figures were all over the place. I didn't feel very tan or fit, and I didn't feel very cute. I felt old and momish. Don't get me wrong, I still try to do what I can to look my best, but age can be very unfriendly to a woman.

Later, at dinner time, Sean noticed I seemed down and asked me about it. I was embarrassed to tell him, but I said, "I just feel old. I look at all these cute girls around me, and my body just doesn't look that way anymore." Without skipping a beat he said, "Babe, those girls don't hold a candle to you. They may look good on the outside, but they've got some developing to do on the inside. I'd pick you over them any day. You're perfect." And then he kissed me on the forehead. Praise the Lord for inner beauty!

You can love your husband, before you even have one, by developing inner beauty.

Key Truth
Don't be concerned about the outward beauty of fancy hairstyles, expensive jewelry, or beautiful clothes. You should clothe yourselves instead with the beauty that comes from within, the unfading beauty of a gentle and quiet spirit, which is so precious to God. 1 Peter 3:3–4

Points to Ponder
Which character bundle are you operating from, Bundle A or Bundle B?

Action Step

Find a woman who demonstrates the character qualities you want to grow in. Ask her how she developed those qualities, and ask if she would be willing to pray for you.

Additional Resource

The Practice of Godliness, Jerry Bridges
This was the first book I ever read on character, and it is my favorite one.

Endnotes

1. Ivory soap slogan was focused primarily on its purity.
2. Merriam-Webster, s.v. "character," https://www.merriam-webster.com/dictionary/character.
3. 1 Peter 3:3–4.
4. www.stitchfix.com.
5. 1 Peter 3:3 (NASB).
6. Source unknown.
7. Galatians 5:22–23.
8. Galatians 5:19–21.
9. 1 Timothy 4:7.
10. 1 Peter 3:4.
11. Kay Arthur gave this definition for "gentleness" in her online lecture of Ephesians 4 through her *Precepts for Life* online Bible study, http://www.precept.org/precepts-for-life/.
12. Gary Hill, *The Discovery Bible* (Chicago: Moody Press, 1987), 532.
13. Luke 6:35.

I lived most of my life with my own agenda — mainly to make myself look better to other people by getting good grades, having a thriving social life, and hopefully attracting a guy along the way. It worked for a little while, but it was a lot to keep up with. When I discovered how I could live for God's purposes, I felt free from trying to impress other people and had a sense of satisfaction that my life had never had before.
— Natalie, twenty-three years old

In three short years of marriage, our lives have changed drastically. We have weathered every transition and change well together, because we started out on the same page. The details have changed, but who we are and what we live for has remained constant.
— Christina, thirty, married at twenty-six

I'm so glad I found a driving purpose for my life before I met my husband. The big-picture purpose that God gave me really narrowed my options for dating. While having even fewer dating options was often discouraging, the reality was that fewer options made dating a lot less difficult. My life purpose allowed clarity and confidence when the right man entered the picture.
— Meredith, thirty-five, married at twenty-nine

6

Paper Clips and Mace

Discover Your Purpose

I imagine that your kitchen has a junk drawer. Almost every kitchen has one. It's the drawer that doesn't really have a purpose, so it gets filled with random things like gum, extra pencils, tape, a nail file, coupons, and paper clips. You just never know what you'll find in there.

During our first year of marriage, Sean found a canister in our junk drawer that he *thought* was mouth freshener spray; he decided he'd freshen up his breath and ended up spraying himself with *mace*! We still laugh over that.

I'm bringing up the junk drawer because I've noticed that some single women live their lives like that drawer. They aren't really intentional about living out a purpose in life, so they end up filling their lives with whatever comes along. Good stuff, but kinda random. The paper clips of life.

Have you ever thought about your purpose in life? If I asked you to write it down right now, would that be easy or hard for you?

In college I was challenged to discover my purpose and mission in life. Steve, the same guy I had heard speak about love, shared with us his concept for making life decisions called *Master, Mission, Mate.*

He talked about how important it is to choose our *Master* first. Someone is directing the decisions we make in life. Who is that for you? Personally, I had lived long enough trying to be in control of my life, and I just couldn't get it right. God made me, and He knew how I worked best. I had recently decided to make Jesus my master. *Check.*

Then he talked about discovering your *Mission.* This is what your life is about, regardless of your career, location, or season of life. He challenged us to think about this question: "If God is our Master, what does He want us to do with our lives?" Whoa. This was a big one, and at the time I couldn't check it off yet.

Finally he said, once you have those in place, then you are in a great spot to look for a *Mate.* When you have the first two decided, that sets you up to find someone who shares your Master and Mission, and you can be a team, working together to accomplish a shared vision for life.

Often people do things in a different order and choose their mate first. By the time they figure out their master and their mission, those may not be in sync with their mate, and that can cause problems. Well I could totally relate to that! I had just experienced the issues that came with choosing a mate before the other two, and it didn't work well at all for me. This talk made total sense, and I decided my next step was to figure out my mission in life.

So how does a girl find her mission in life?

I had a guy friend who once said that he needed to "find himself" so he went off to Europe. I had already been to Europe. It was an incredible trip, and I took a lot of pictures, but there were no huge personal revelations for me while I was there. I learned a lot about myself from what God had to say in the Bible, so that's where I chose to look. I spent time thinking about Steve's question: "If God is my Master, what does He want me to do with my life?" I dug into my Bible, searching for answers.

If I was going to be concerned about what mattered to God, I figured I should prioritize making disciples.

As a single woman, this verse caught my attention:

A woman who is no longer married or has never been married can be devoted to the Lord and holy in body and in spirit.[1]

It became my aim to be devoted to God and to be concerned about things important to Him. Since following God is a relationship, I looked for ways to know Him better and to have a closer relationship with Him. I joined a Bible study. I kept reading my Bible and praying each day. I began memorizing Bible verses. Getting to know God and learning to love Him was bringing more clarity and purpose to my life.

Jesus's last instructions to His followers also gained my attention:

Jesus came and told his disciples,
"I have been given all authority in heaven and on
earth. Therefore, go and make disciples of all the

*nations, baptizing them in the name of the Father and
the Son and the Holy Spirit. Teach these new disciples
to obey all the commands I have given you."*[2]

If I was going to be concerned about what mattered
to God, I figured I should prioritize making disciples. A
disciple is a follower of Christ, so I did my best to be a
disciple myself. I started putting into practice all that I
learned from the Bible. I needed help knowing how to
live it all out, so an older believer started spending time
with me each week to help me grow. I enjoyed building
relationships with believers on campus who also wanted to
make disciples. I joined a church community, which gave
me relationships with older believers who could teach me.
I got baptized like Jesus said to do. I began praying for my
family and the people around me.

I knew being a disciple also meant making disciples.
Making disciples is loving the people around you and
helping them begin and grow in their relationships with
God. As a student, I started having spiritual conversations
with my friends. Not all were interested, but some were!
Kristen was interested, so we started spending time together
talking about the Bible and praying for each other and for
our friends. Together, we invited them to the campus Bible
study, and I even started one in our sorority. As a fairly shy
introvert, it was challenging to take initiative in others' lives
spiritually. I probably wasn't the best at it, but I didn't give
up. It was pretty awesome to see God work in my friends'
lives. I was learning to love others and make disciples, and
it was very fulfilling. God's mission of making disciples was
becoming my purpose.

I also began to learn about the "nations" Jesus talked
about. I took a class at church called *Perspectives* with some

of my friends.[3] The Bible says, "God so loved the world," and in that course we learned what God was doing around the world.[4] I couldn't believe there were so many groups of people who didn't have someone who could tell them how they could find God's forgiveness. Some of these groups did not even have access to a Bible in their language. *What would I have done without a Bible or someone to help me understand how to have a relationship with God?* That didn't seem fair, and I wanted to do my part to give them the opportunities I had been given. It didn't take long before I was on a plane to serve people in one of the nations I had read about.

When I came home, I decided that no matter what my job or profession was, whether I was single or married, with kids or not, I wanted my life to be devoted to God. I wanted to make disciples, and I wanted it to make a difference that touched lives here and abroad.

There are some good things He has prepared in advance for you to do.

I had discovered my mission.

God actually asks everyone who wants to follow Him to devote themselves to loving and knowing Him and to help others know Him too.[5] Although followers of Christ might all have the same overarching mission from our Master, the individual roles we play in fulfilling this mission can look very different based on our unique designs.

For we are God's masterpiece. He has created us anew in Christ Jesus, so we can do the good things he planned for us long ago.[6]

This verse says that you are His masterpiece. He designed you. He crafted *you*. He made *you*. There are some good things He has prepared in advance for *you* to do. He's already thought it through. Blows my mind. No random paper clips here.

Also, not only has He built you for a special work and prepared it all in advance, but if you are a believer in Him, He has empowered you in a special way to do that very work. The Bible says, when you believe in Him, God's Spirit comes inside of you, and He gives you a gift, something that is supernatural. This gift is referred to in the Bible as a "spiritual gift."[7] It's kinda like a superpower to help you pull off the work He has prepared for you to do. I mean, who doesn't want a superpower?

Figuring out your unique design is fun and can help you find a great fit in fulfilling God's big picture of making disciples of all nations. Not only do we all have gifts to help us do the specific work He has prepared for us, but we also have certain groups of people we naturally want to spend time with and help. Regardless of our career path, position, or season of life, we can all play a role in God's mission.

As I was evaluating where my gifts and passions best fit in fulfilling God's mission, I was given an opportunity to work full-time in campus ministry, making disciples among college students. It seemed like a great direction for me, but making disciples doesn't mean you have to go into full-time ministry. Many of the young women I have discipled through the years have gone into various other professions and are following God's mission of making disciples. Here are a few of their stories:

Kristen, whom I mentioned earlier, is the driving force behind missions in her church. She has helped take teams into many different countries, some countries that I have never stepped foot in.

She and her husband have done training with church leaders all over the world. Her heart beats for the nations to know about Jesus.

Susan became a successful accountant in a large company. In the evenings and on weekends, she discipled high school girls. Years ago, I was visiting with a young mom in our church, only to discover that when she was in high school, Susan had led her to Christ. Even though I didn't know this young mom well, I was her spiritual grandma! Susan, like me, got married in her thirties. She and her husband met on a mission trip to Honduras. After years in the business world, they now work in youth ministry, providing opportunities for more young people to hear about Jesus.

Pam is one of the most popular designers in our area, and her work is often highlighted in local magazines. She loves helping women create homes they love, and these women become her friends, not just clients. Her husband, Clark, is a pastor at my church. Together they do a lot of premarital counseling with young couples, and she disciples the young wives who are in her Bible study.

Living for God's mission gave their lives and marriages an eternal element because they were living for something bigger together.

I always knew Heather was spunky, but I had no idea that she would end up being the mom of seven kids—six boys! She's launching out blonde-headed disciples who all have her last name.

She homeschools them all, so it's a wonder she has time for anything else, but she is also involved in an outreach to teen moms. Their whole family has opened their house as a "home away from home" for two young women from Kenya.

I enjoyed living out my purpose in life, and I wanted a mate someday who not only shared God's mission of making disciples of all nations but also whose purpose I could partner with. As I watched other couples around me, the marriages I admired had a common purpose beyond their marriage. They were a team, serving God together. Their passions and giftings were in sync, complementing rather than competing with each other. Living for God's mission gave their lives and marriages an eternal element because they were living for something bigger together. I wanted a teammate like that.

Of course these were *totally* the extra challenges my dating life needed. So there I was in small town USA, as a six-foot-one, thirty-year-old single woman looking for someone who shared my heart for God and for making disciples. Unless God intervened, my dating options were looking *pretty slim*.

My church community made it their mission to help me, so they often introduced me to their single nephew... or friend...or neighbor. They were thoughtful and meant well, so I had some blind dates. I quickly learned how to transition conversation to life purpose. I would regularly ask my blind dates, *"So what do you see as your purpose in life?"* I figured my future husband would appreciate the topic, but in the meantime that discussion *definitely* weeded out some guys.

There is an illustration that describes this season that

I heard from a pastor, Tommy Nelson. He said, as you are running the race of life, living according to God's mission and His design for you, you should look beside you on the road and see who is running next to you. Those are the people whose lives and passions will be most in sync with yours.

When Sean came around, we were already doing a lot of the same things. The way we were living our lives was already in sync. I guess you could say I looked next to me on the road and there he was! On our first date, he brought up the life purpose topic before I even had to ask. I admired his values and the way he pursued God's mission.

Our passions, gifts, and purposes worked well together. I realized whatever profession he or I chose, and wherever life took us, I could see myself as a teammate with him.

When you and your mate are both living for an eternal purpose, it can take teamwork in your marriage to a deeper level. Together we are a team in raising our family and discipling our kids. There are times I might be at home with the kids while Sean is out meeting with students, but because we are a team in our mission, we share in the wins of students growing spiritually. He might be at home with the kids while I'm away finishing up this book, but we are a team, and we share the win.

Even though we have very different gifts, they are similar enough that they work well together. When he uses his gifts to do the things God has called him to do, sometimes I am right beside him, and we are doing the same thing. Other times I am cheering for him, in his corner, supporting him as he lives out God's design for his life. He does the same for me. Finding our missions first, and then marrying a mate whose purpose lined up with ours, has made it possible for us each to do the good works

God planned for us with the support of a loving teammate by our side.

You can love your husband, before you even have one, by discovering God's purpose for your life and choosing a husband whose purpose works well with yours.

Key Truth

I have been given all authority in heaven and on earth. Therefore, go and make disciples of all the nations, baptizing them in the name of the Father and the Son and the Holy Spirit. Teach these new disciples to obey all the commands I have given you. Matthew 28:18–20a

Points to Ponder

If God is your Master, what is His purpose for you?

Action Step

If you already know your purpose, write it out. If you don't, take a step toward discovering it.

Additional Resources

The Purpose Driven Life, Rick Warren
Sean and I both really like this book.

Disciples Are Made, Not Born, Walter A. Henrichsen
This book impacted me tremendously in college.

www.thetravelingteam.org

Learn about what God is doing around the world from this incredible group.

www.joshuaproject.net

Find out about nations who still need to hear about Jesus. I use their app to pray for an unreached people group every day.

Endnotes

1. 1 Corinthians 7:34.

2. Matthew 28:18–20.

3. Perspectives on the World Christian Movement, www.perspectives. org.

4. John 3:16 (NIV).

5. Matthew 22:37–40.

6. Ephesians 2:10.

7. Ephesians 1:13; Romans 12:6; 1 Corinthians 12:4–11.

Marriage is meant to be fun, super romantic, and your goal is to make each other happy. [Your spouse] should fulfill your every need (even if they don't know it), and if they can't then you shouldn't be with them. The goal is to stay together, but if you don't there's always a way out like divorce or something. If they don't make you happy or provide for you (physically, mentally, and maybe spiritually, if you're into that) then something is wrong with the relationship. The man should make a bunch of money and/or the wife because she is a strong, independent woman too. So both make money and work full-time, so that y'all can do cool things together, have a secure and comfortable life, with romance constantly flowing and maybe to also be able to provide for kids one day, if you want them.
Marriage is best when I look at it with the mindset "Is this what is best for ME and MY life right now?"
—College Student (who needs to read this chapter)

———————

Giving in to your emotional cravings through romantic movies, books, etc. breeds discontentment in marriage as well as in single life.
—Wife, married two years

———————

Marriage doesn't fix everything.
—Wife, married one year

7

Box Office Flops

Build Realistic Expectations

When I was very single and everyone around me was falling in love and getting married, I sometimes wrote short love letters to my unknown, hoped for, future husband as a way to deal with all the different emotions I felt. I poured out my heart and told him how much I looked forward to when God would bring us together. It wasn't something I did a lot, just when things were really hard for me during my season of singleness. I only had five letters, and I kept them tucked away in my journals. They were treasures to me, and I could not wait to share them with my husband someday. It would let him know that I was thinking of him as I waited.

Aren't stories like this what the best romance movies are made of? I even let myself daydream that if my love life was ever made into a movie, *The Letters* would be a perfect title for it.

When Sean and I got engaged, I quickly pulled out those letters from my old journals. I was eager for him to have them, but I chose not to tell him about them right away. I decided the most magical moment to give them to him would be the night before our wedding day. *Oh, that would be perfect.* I planned it all out in my mind.

After our rehearsal dinner, I gave him the precious letters all tied up in a pretty ribbon. We said sweet words to each other and then parted ways. I left to attend my lingerie party with my bridesmaids, and Sean was off to play basketball with his groomsmen. I could not wait to talk to him about them on our honeymoon. *How much more romantic could this be? I wrote him letters when I didn't even know him. I wonder if he wrote letters to me too?* It seemed so dreamy as I crawled into bed by myself for the very last time.

I woke up to my long-awaited wedding day, and as expected it was busy with flurries of activity—getting ready, seeing family and friends, taking pictures. I didn't even eat much that day much less think about the letters.

We begin longing for something that isn't even real.

On our first morning as husband and wife, Sean whisked me away to a surprise-to-me destination on an island in the Pacific Northwest. On our second day there, as we were curled up together on the couch, the timing seemed perfect. I sweetly asked him, "So what did you think of my letters?"

"What letters?"

"The letters I gave to you after the rehearsal dinner. You know, the ones I wrote to you before I even knew you."

"Oh no, Kim. I think I left them at the gym." His face dropped, "I am so sorry, but I didn't get to read them."

I sat there stunned. *Did I just hear him right? He lost my letters? He never even read them?*

Well that would never happen in a movie.

Romantic movie, meet real life. Real life, meet romantic movie. It was an awkward introduction on day two of our honeymoon.

Often we enter marriage with a fairy-tale perspective that our life and relationship will be like the romantic movies we watch. When a chick flick we want to see finally comes out, we round up our girlfriends and head to the theater. We buy our bucket of popcorn and our Diet Cokes and grab the best seats. As the big screen flashes its images in front of us, we sit there with our hearts wide open and our mouths full of popcorn. We laugh, we cry, we feel giddy and angry and all the other feels throughout the course of two hours. By the time the credits roll, our eyes are all sparkly, and our hearts are crying out, "That's what I want!"

Although our brains know it, our longing hearts don't stop to consider that the movie is...PRETEND! It's made up. It's fiction. The people in it are only acting. The writer of that movie, which perfectly depicts our dream romance, could have easily been a single, middle-aged lady, who has a ton of cats and hasn't had a date in years. While she sipped boxed wine and snacked on Cheetos, *she made the whole story up*. We allow ourselves to forget that the movie we are watching is make-believe, and we let our hearts entertain the idea that our lives will be like that one day. We begin longing for something that *isn't even real*.

After we get married, it doesn't take long to realize that our marriage is not like that movie at all. Bae would rather watch the NBA finals than dance with me on an abandoned street? *How can this be?* We start comparing our reality to something that was a pretend story from the beginning, and we are left disappointed.

Fairy-tale relationships began to lose their enchantment over me, and healthy, realistic ones took their place.

The truth is, more often than not, movies do not provide a realistic picture of what good marriages look like. In my earlier years, I got all my ideas about love from the movies, and they were a terrible source of information for me. As a result, I made some pretty foolish choices.

I remember when I first came to grips with the truth about movies in college. My favorite movie at that time involved a man who felt an unexplainable, magnetic connection to a woman in a photograph who lived in the era before him. He was so consumed with her that he figured out a way to travel through time to find her. I thought it was the best love story ever, and to this day hearing its familiar melody will stop me in my tracks.

When I began to realize that my life would never be like a movie, a brief period of grief followed. I had to accept the harsh reality that my one-and-only soul mate would not travel through time to find me.[1] Watching my favorite love story just wasn't the same after that. Silly laws of physics. They were completely spoiling my romantic hopes and dreams.

As painful as this process of discovery was, it was actually quite healthy for me and my future marriage. Fairy-tale relationships began to lose their enchantment over me, and healthy, realistic ones took their place.

I began to get good information about what love and marriage were really about, and it began reshaping my views of what a real marriage looked like.

If you want to love your husband, before you even have one, you need to build realistic expectations in love and marriage. You need an honest picture of what marriage is supposed to be. Believe me, if you enter marriage with the right expectations, you and your husband will be much happier!

If you enter marriage with wrong ideas of what love and marriage are supposed to be, these unrealistic expectations will leave you continually disappointed. In fact, unrealistic and unmet expectations rank in "The Top 10 Reasons Marriages Fail" on Divorce.com.[2]

So where do you get *good* information about marriage?

Here is a working definition of marriage for you:

> *Marriage is when a selfish, imperfect man and a selfish, imperfect woman, who are different from each other, learn to love and care for one another, and function together as a team.*

Reading those books wasn't as fun as watching chick flicks, but they helped me enter marriage with a much more realistic view of what it was going to be like.

There is a lot more to marriage of course, but honestly this is a very real description of my day-to-day, happily-married-for-twenty-years life. It's messy. Sean and I often flop at this. Sometimes there are sweet feelings. Sometimes there are angry ones. Sometimes we laugh. Sometimes I cry. We see both the good and ugly sides of each other. We ask forgiveness. We try again. We stick it out. Sometimes we get it right. When we do get it right, it is sweet and worth what it took to figure it out. Each year we get better at loving and caring for one another.

While the letter debacle may have caught me a little off guard, I entered marriage with pretty realistic expectations. During my single years, I was able to build some friendships with several older married women who were trying to do things God's way. I heard their stories and saw their lives. I began to piece together the realities of a good marriage, and the picture of marriage I formed was very different from the movies. I would sometimes walk away from time with them thinking, *Whew, I am so glad I am single*. I was creating a healthy, accurate view of marriage. To be honest, my new understanding of marriage would have made a pretty boring movie.

Did you know that the Bible tells older godly women to teach the younger women to love their husbands?[3] It does. There was a time when I had no idea that I needed to be taught how to love my husband. But I came to realize that something was always influencing me. I just had to decide if I was going to be taught from fairy tales or reality. I am so thankful for the older married women I spent time with. I learned so much, and I have a better marriage because of them.

I also read a few good books on marriage while I was single. I was in my late twenties when my parents divorced, and my dad gave me three books on marriage for Christmas that year. I quickly read them all, because I was ready and eager to learn from their mistakes. I'll be honest, after reading one of them about how different men and women and their needs are, I thought being single wasn't so bad after all. Reading those books wasn't as fun as watching chick flicks, but they helped me enter marriage with a much more realistic view of what it was going to be like.

And, of course, the Bible is filled with some incredible insights about relationships and marriage. During my single years, I learned quite a bit about what God had to say about marriage by studying the Bible myself and hearing people teach about marriage from the Bible.

Because of godly women, relationship books, and the Bible, I was aware of the realities of a good marriage. I knew that it wasn't like the movies. I knew better, but somehow my expectations about the letters slipped right on through.

I had an expectation that Sean would treasure those letters as much as I did. I also had an expectation that the letters would be a romantic moment of connection between us. However, it was not playing out like I had pictured in my mind at all. I was on the brink of being disappointed two days into marriage!

I took a deep breath. *He left them at the gym without ever reading them?* My brain was racing. An image of a janitor opening and reading my precious letters filled my mind, but that was interrupted by imagining a junior high boy who found them with his friends! *Wait, was my name on them anywhere?* My heart sank at the thought that whoever found them probably just tossed my treasured love letters into the gym's smelly garbage can.

In a matter of seconds, the battle between realistic and unrealistic expectations was on. I took another deep breath and quickly processed the situation in my mind as rationally as I could. Those letters had served their purpose to help me get through the difficulties of being single.

To be fair to Sean, I had not emphasized to him ahead of time how special those letters were to me. Also, I had given them to him when he was distracted and busy. I was on my dream, surprise-destination honeymoon with the wonderful husband I had waited for. Did I feel loved? *Yes*. So did I really need those letters? *No*. Sean felt loved, and he obviously did not *need* those letters either. Disappointment loomed for that moment, but I was not going to let it be a downer for my entire honeymoon.

In the end, realistic expectations trumped the fairy tale, and I decided to just let it go. I finally responded, "Aw, Babe, are you serious? I'm so disappointed. Those letters were special to me because I wrote them to you before I knew who you were." He apologized again and held me. I was able to move on, and we enjoyed the rest of our honeymoon. It's tragic to think of what I would have missed out on had my heart kept pining for the pretend.

You can love your husband, before you even have one, by gaining realistic expectations about what love and marriage are actually like.

Key Truth
These older women must train the younger women to love their husbands. Titus 2:4a

Points to Ponder
Have you been learning about love and marriage mainly from movies and romance novels, or are you getting a realistic picture from other sources?

Action Steps

Initiate spending time with an older married woman around you who is trying to live life God's way. Take her out to lunch. (If she has young kids, offer to take some lunch to her.) Here are some possible questions to ask to get you started:

- Has marriage been different from your original expectations?
- If so, in what way?
- What advice would you have for me?

Additional Resources

Things I Wish I'd Known Before We Got Married,
Gary Chapman
Great book. Easy read. Lots of helpful insights on the realities of marriage.

The Meaning of Marriage, Timothy Keller
Also a great book. Goes a little deeper.

Endnotes

1. Ironically, Jesus did travel through time to find me.
2. "Top 10 Reasons Marriages Fail," *Divorce.com*, http://divorce.com/top-10-reasons-marriages-fail/.
3. Titus 2:4.

I dated a guy, and we would talk about our life together after we got married. Where we were going to live, how our careers would mesh, how many kids we were going to have. When we broke up, I didn't know what my life was going to look like anymore. I had already planned my life with this guy, and I didn't know how I was supposed to do it without him.
It left me heart broken and confused.
—**Morgan, twenty-one years old**

———————

I am so thankful I practiced discipline with my thoughts when I was single, because it helps so much in marriage. For someone who was pretty disciplined at it, it is still a struggle, so I'm really glad I worked on it before marriage!
—**Wife, thirty-three, married three years**

———————

I never realized the unhealthy patterns I developed while dating wouldn't automatically change when I got married.
—**Wife, married five years**

8

Catching Feelings

Guard Your Heart

M y friend sat across from me in the booth, and we
chatted freely like usual. Then he glanced down
to grab the straw wrapper on the table. As he wrapped it
around his finger, he looked up and said, "Kim, Meghan
and I are dating now."[1] It wasn't a complete surprise, but
my heart still felt stabbed. I tried my best to maintain my
composure and not show how much it hurt.

My heart felt those stabbing pains all over again years
later when another close friend told me about his new
girlfriend. *Would I ever learn?* After they got engaged, she
actually called me for advice because I "understood him so
well." I remember thinking, *I don't think it's supposed to be
this way. I hope when I get married someday there's not a girl
out there who knows my husband better than I do.*

As a single woman, I had multiple opportunities to
learn some hard lessons about how to interact with my

male friends. In both of these instances, I allowed my heart to get too attached to someone, and it really hurt when they didn't choose me. To top it off, I had a front-row seat to watch their new romances. My poor heart. I had to figure this out, or I wouldn't survive singleness well at all.

Have you heard of this Bible verse before?

Guard your heart above all else,
for it determines the course of your life.[2]

When I first heard it, I was all for it. Clearly my heart needed protecting. However it didn't take long for me to ask, *What in the world does that mean? How do I do that?*

A young friend of mine recently told me that she was very annoyed when she first heard the phrase, "guard your heart." If you aren't all for it, that's OK, but let's explore what it means. In this chapter, I'll do my best to share what I have learned, and we'll unpack this concept of guarding your heart to help you navigate the crazy emotions of relationships.

It should be normal and expected to not act on every feeling we have.

Guarding your heart doesn't just apply to dating relationships, but that will be our focus here. And, sadly, I can make no guarantees that if you follow my advice your heart will never get hurt, but I do think there are some precautions you can take and skills you can learn to help protect yourself.

Often we are told by the culture around us to "Follow your heart!" and "Do what you feel!" This sounds somewhat noble at first: *Why deny what's in your heart?* But it doesn't work. What will you do in marriage when your husband is driving you crazy and you *feel* like killing him?

Did you know the Bible even says that our hearts can trick us sometimes?

The heart is deceitful above all things and beyond cure.
Who can understand it? [3]

Because of this, we shouldn't fully trust our hearts or let them lead us. If we do, we may end up somewhere we never intended or wanted to be.

Our culture also makes it seem like it's the worst thing ever to deny ourselves the desires that are in our heart, but Jesus told people that to follow Him meant denying themselves.[4] It should be normal and expected to not act on every feeling we have.

Let's go back to our main verse. Here's another Bible study insight. If you look up the word *heart* in the original language you'll find that the heart is *not* just our feelings and passions, but it includes our thoughts as well. The word refers to that place inside of us where our thoughts and feelings live. It's the seat of emotions, *and* intellect, *and* thinking.[5] This is huge.

Thankfully, our hearts are more than feelings. It's hard to control our feelings, but we can control our thoughts. Now sometimes we might not think we can control our thoughts, but we can. The Bible says we can change the way we think.

Don't copy the behavior and customs of this world,
but let God transform you into a new person
by changing the way you think. [6]

You can change the way you think.
Have you ever noticed how our minds can often take

bits and pieces of information and create pretend scenarios in our head that aren't even real? One of my friends tells a funny story of how she began thinking about a random guy in one of her classes, and before she knew it she had dreamed about what it would be like to be married to him and had designed their family Christmas card!

The good news is that we are not just helpless against these feelings.

Thoughts like that may seem harmless and fun, but if you continue to think about them and create the pretend scenarios in your head, those thoughts will affect your feelings and emotions, especially toward that person. You may start developing feelings and creating expectations, and your heart may get attached to a scenario that was never true.

$$\textit{Thoughts} \longrightarrow \textit{Feelings} \longrightarrow \textit{Actions}$$

Our thoughts are what create those feelings and emotions in us, and together they determine the actions we take. Although we may not be able to immediately change our feelings, we can eventually influence our feelings by controlling what we choose to think about. The good news is that we are not just helpless against these feelings. We are able to guard our hearts.

Let's talk about *guard*. Guard means to watch over and gives the idea of a *blockade*.[7] You *watch over* and *blockade* things you are trying to protect. When you are protecting something, you recognize that not everything is good for it. Not everything is welcome.

The picture that pops into my head when I think of *guard* is the guard at the gated community of some friends of ours. We can't just drive up to their house freely. We always have to stop by the guard in the hut and say, "Hi. We're the Vollendorfs. We'd like to go see the Robinsons." The guard on duty has to give us an OK and open the gate before we can go in.

I would like to propose to you that "guarding your heart" is not too complicated. It's posting a guard on what we allow in our heart by being careful about what we *choose to keep thinking about*. Since I can't control my feelings very easily, I'm careful about what thoughts I let in and keep thinking about, because I know those thoughts will ultimately influence my feelings.

Not every thought that pops into my mind is allowed to stay there. When a thought shows up, I have a choice:

Do I keep thinking about this? or
Will I intentionally start thinking about
something else?

Two of the requirements for a thought to get past the guard of my heart is that the thought has to be *true* and *pure*.

Let's talk about *true* thoughts first. Only the thoughts that are true get an OK to enter in and dwell in my mind. If a thought is not true, I won't let it through, no matter how many times it shows up at the guard hut and asks to come in.

Perhaps an example will help.

When Sean first called and asked me to have dinner with him, I was giddy with excitement. Thoughts began quickly popping up in my mind. *I wonder if he likes me. He must like me since he wants to spend time with me...Is he the ONE?* By this time I had figured out the guard idea, so I made a choice to control what I kept thinking about. I took a deep breath and asked myself, "Kim, what's true

"Kim, what's true right now?"

right now?" The truth was that Sean Vollendorf wanted to spend some time with me. That's all I knew. I didn't know why, and I didn't know his intentions, so the only thought I allowed myself to keep thinking about was that a neat man like Sean Vollendorf wanted to spend some time with me. That alone was a happy thought.

When Sean asked me out again, the same thoughts pulled up at the "gate" in my mind. *OK, so he totally likes you! What if you guys get married?* I'd have to go through the same process. *OK, Kim, what's true?* The only true thing was that he must have had an enjoyable time and wanted to spend more time with me. That was the only thought I'd allow myself to think about. I could enjoy the thought that such a neat man wanted to spend more time with me, but I would choose not to dwell on thoughts that went past that. Thoughts like, *I wonder how I would sign my name if I was Kim Vollendorf?* got shut down.

I love having friends, but sometimes they can be the worst when you are trying to keep your thoughts limited to what is true. "You guys went out again? Omg! I bet you guys will be married this summer!" Girls love relationships and dream of romance. It is tempting, especially when talking with your girlfriends, to start analyzing the situation and create a scenario that most likely doesn't even exist. When Sean and I were dating, I remember telling myself and a friend, "I'll believe that he likes me when he tells me himself, and not before."

It's a learned skill, and when you are single is a great time to practice it.

And here's a bonus lesson I learned. Even when Sean later told me that he liked me and wanted to date me, I asked a few clarifying questions: *So what do you mean by "dating"? What do you think that would look like for us?* Once a guy I was seriously dating told me that he was a "one woman man." Now I don't know what you think when you hear that, but I thought he meant that I was the "one woman" for him. I let myself create scenarios and expectations in my heart. Well, he later told me that he meant he would only date one girl at a time. *Ohhh...* well, as a result of our very painful breakup, I learned to ask questions along the way to make sure I understood what was true.

This whole process can be a bit tedious, but it kept my heart in check, and it didn't allow my feelings to go wild and unrestrained like they had in the past. It takes a vigilant effort to keep our thoughts based on what is really true. It's a learned skill, and when you are single is a great time to practice it.

I would have been disappointed if Sean and I hadn't continued toward marriage, but I wouldn't have been devastated. I hadn't decorated our living room. I hadn't picked out my bridesmaids. I hadn't designed our Christmas card. I let myself fully enjoy each new stage of our relationship as it came, but not before.

> *If you allow yourself to think about the wrong things, eventually you'll be tempted to do the wrong things.*

Guarding your heart totally pays off! If you can learn to stay in the here and now and not live in an alternate reality you've created in your mind, your life will be so much less awkward now and later. Let me tell you something, these guys you are spending time with don't really go away. Sean is friends with some of the guys I "spent time" with. I also have a friend whose old boyfriend lived right next door to her! Right. Next. Door.

Not only do thoughts have to be *true* to get past the guard of my heart, they also have to be *pure*. I make an intentional effort to not continue thinking about thoughts that aren't pure.

As a single woman, the most random sexual things would pop into my mind, but I learned to say, *Nope. Not going there.* Then I would tell myself something true like, *I'm sure glad God knows what's best for me.* This is where Scripture memory comes in handy. Here are some true things I learned from the Bible that were great "substitute thoughts" when I needed them:

*The LORD will withhold no good thing
from those who do what is right.*[8]

*[God's plans are] for good and not for disaster,
to give you a future and a hope.*[9]

*Fix your thoughts on what is true, and honorable,
and right, and pure, and lovely, and admirable. Think
about things that are excellent and worthy of praise.*[10]

If you allow yourself to go places in your mind and dwell on thoughts that aren't pure, then fighting for purity will be a lot more difficult. If you allow yourself to think about the wrong things, eventually you'll be tempted to do the wrong things.

Thoughts ⟶ *Feelings* ⟶ *Actions*

We may try to rationalize that since we're *only thinking* about it that it's OK. But eventually those thoughts feed our feelings. Then we start responding emotionally and physically, and it gets tougher to maintain self-control and stay pure. This is why I avoid certain movies and books. After watching or reading them, all kinds of thoughts show up, and those thoughts invite other thoughts. Next thing I know I have an army of thoughts I don't want to be thinking beating down the guard hut of my heart. Fighting them off can be an exhausting battle. It's just easier to avoid watching or reading stuff like that in the first place.

Addictions complicate this process. If we have let certain pornographic or erotic images in over and over again, it's like they become bullies and refuse to respect a blockade. The more they have had access, the harder it gets to start turning them away. When dealing with addictions, we often have to call in reinforcements. I've listed some helpful resources at the end of the chapter.

Another lesson I have learned (the hard way) is that our guard needs to keep tabs on how much time we spend with someone. It may even be a beneficial friend, but if you continue spending time with someone, building memories, and becoming super familiar with them without any type of mutual commitment, someone's heart will get attached. It's just how it works. It doesn't mean you can't spend time with a guy, but if over the course of a few months you are continually doing things together without a definition, one of you will get attached.

When I was single, I began to pray for the future wife of my friend or crush. Praying for their future spouse will keep your heart in check real quick because you'll be continually reminding yourself that it might not be you. If that's easy for you to do, then you're probably OK, but if it gets difficult, you may need to re-evaluate your friendship with him.

One of the problems with these undefined friendships

is that they could actually hinder relationships with better suited guys that might come along. If you feel really comfortable with your current guy friend, you might not be as interested if some other guy comes around. Likewise, a guy who might be interested in you could see a friendship like that and assume you are a couple. It's important to not be all tied up with the wrong guy. You need to be emotionally free for the right one.

You might be surprised that guarding my heart is a skill that I still use.

When I started learning this, I even had to say to a guy, "I enjoy spending time with you, but since we are going to be 'just friends' I won't be able to spend as much time with you. I need to move on emotionally." This wasn't an easy decision, but it was the right one. As time and my heart eventually moved on, a young man named Sean Vollendorf called me. I am so thankful I had put some distance emotionally between me and the other guy.

I'm glad that I learned this skill of guarding my heart while I was single. I've had some time to build up this muscle, and the guard of my mind is pretty beefy. You might be surprised that guarding my heart is a skill that I still use. Temptations don't just go away when you get married.

I heard the story recently of a married woman who had multiple affairs, and she ripped her family apart. Her husband tried to stay with her for the sake of the kids, but her heart continued to wander. She had never learned to guard her heart, and it led her to a place she—and her family—didn't want to be.

The same process I went through as a single woman is the process I use as a married woman. I still interact with other men, and I need to be guarded in my interactions with and thoughts about them. When crazy random thoughts pop up in my mind, I'm used to dealing with them. They don't get in. Instead, truth and purity have filled my heart, and they've allowed my heart to guide the course of my life well. I am grateful.

You can love your husband, before you even have one, by learning to guard your heart.

Key Truth
Guard your heart above all else, for it determines the course of your life. Proverbs 4:23

Points to Ponder
What would your life be like if you only allowed in thoughts that were true and pure?

Action Steps
Start this process by writing down recurring thoughts that fill your mind. Ask yourself if they are true and pure.

Start praying for the future spouses of all your guy friends, and see how your heart responds.

Additional Resources
Good Pictures, Bad Pictures
Kristen A. Jenson, MA and Gail Poyner, PhD
This is a children's book, but it is one of the best I've read to understand how addictions work—pornography in particular.

www.TheFreedomFight.org
This program was started by a colleague of mine. There is a "Sexual Addiction Screening Test" available on this website, which can help determine your need.

Sexual Sanity for Women, Ellen Dykas

Behind the Mask, Rebecca Bradley and Diane Roberts, www.puredesire.org

Eight Pillars to Freedom from Love Addiction and Sexual Issues, www.puredesire.org

www.rtribe.com

*These are all resources that my colleagues and I have used through the years to help our students deal with sexual addictions. You might consult an older believer who is helping you grow spiritually to help you determine which one is the best fit for you. Some of these are more effective used in a small group setting. In some cases, professional counseling is the next step to take, but these resources can get you started in the right direction.

Endnotes

1. Not her real name.

2. Proverbs 4:23.

3. Jeremiah 17:9 (NIV).

4. Luke 9:23 (HCSB). *Then [Jesus] said to them all, "If anyone wants to come with Me, he must deny himself, take up his cross daily, and follow me."*

5. *Bible Study Tools*, s.v. "heart," http://www.biblestudytools.com/dictionary/heart/.

6. Romans 12:2.

7. *Blue Letter Bible*, s.v. "guard," https://www.blueletterbible.org/lang/lexicon/lexicon.cfm?Strongs=H5341&t=NASB.

8. Psalm 84:11.

9. Jeremiah 29:11.

10. Philippians 4:8.

Many single girls assume that only a man can fulfill their deepest desires to be known, cared for, and valued. Through personal experience, I have learned that no man can fill the void of contentment. Knowing God and who He is creates an indescribable intimacy that brings contentment no man could ever or should ever fulfill.

—**Alyssa, twenty-one years old**

I became a believer my junior year of college, after twenty years of allowing the world to negatively shape my view of God and myself. Once I let God into the most intimate places of my heart, He started to tear down the lies I believed, and He began to reveal Himself to me. Even though I still battle the chatter that previously shaped my perception of God, the more I know Him, the more I love Him. God fiercely pursued me to offer redemption, security, hope, and a perfect and constant love. Now I get the chance to fight to intimately know and love Him more and more every day.

—**Becky, twenty-three years old**

There is strength and security in our marriage that can only come from knowing God and His character well. Knowing and believing that God is the ultimate caretaker of my heart, my provider, and the One who meets my every need allows me to look at my husband as a gift and not expect him to be my perfect savior.

—**Jen, forty-one, married sixteen years**

9

Into-Me-See

Know God Well

As a new believer in Christ, I actually looked forward to going to church. I enjoyed growing in my relationship with God and took advantage of the opportunities I had to learn more about Him. One particular Sunday morning, we had a husband and wife come speak to our college class. The guys moved into a different room to hear the husband speak, and the girls all stayed together in the main room to hear from the wife. I have no memory of what she was *actually* speaking on, because I found myself stuck on one phrase she said early in her talk. It completely rocked my world:

"My most intimate moments have not been with a man, but with God."

Now don't get me wrong, I enjoyed my new relationship with God. I enjoyed the forgiveness I experienced, and I enjoyed learning more about Him. But *intimacy?* Intimacy *with God?* Intimacy that *surpassed* what you could experience with a *man?* I didn't hear anything else she said. I sat back in my chair, arms crossed, eyebrows furrowed, mind racing. *Now how in the world does that work? How can a woman experience intimacy with God whom she can neither see nor touch? And to a depth that exceeds what she could experience with a man?*

It is our deepest desire to be wanted and known.

Well it's been more than thirty years since that Sunday morning, and I've been growing in my relationship with God ever since—twelve years as a single woman and twenty years as a married one. You know what, she was right. I agree with her. As much as I enjoy the intimacy I share with my husband, my most intimate moments have not been with him. They've been with God.

The best definition I've heard for intimacy is "into-me-see." It sums up the meaning quite nicely. It is our deepest desire to be wanted and known. We want someone to get to know the real us, and we want to feel valuable and special to that person. We long to feel free to be ourselves, yet still be loved and accepted. We want to feel safe, knowing that he won't hurt us or betray us. We long to be secure, knowing he won't go away when he discovers more of who we really are. We desire to feel valued, cared for, and worth something to someone.

When we are in a relationship like that, it tends to bring out the best version of who we are because we can reveal our complete selves without fear of rejection. Being deeply loved and accepted in this way is extremely rare, and if we find someone who loves us like that, he becomes our everything. He becomes our favorite person to be with. We want to know all we can about him. We find we can't stop thinking about him, and we talk about him all the time. A relationship like that changes us. He becomes our greatest treasure, and we love him back fiercely.

That's intimacy.

We long for intimacy like this, and we assume we'll find it in a relationship with the right guy. When a guy notices us and takes interest in us, we hope that he'll be the one who will love us intimately. Sometimes we even go straight to sex, trying to experience the intimacy we crave. Hoping to win his heart, we'll do anything for what we think is love. But sin and selfishness cause these relationships to fall short of what we hoped they would be. When they disappoint and hurt us, we tell ourselves that there must be someone else better out there, and we keep trying to find him.

What if this craving to be fully known was like a homing device, planted inside of us, to guide us back home... back to Him?

But what if this longing for intimacy was never designed to be completely satisfied in a relationship with a person?

What if this craving to be fully known is like a homing device, planted inside of us, to guide us back home...back to Him?

What if it isn't a "him" we are looking for, but "Him" instead?

Dr. Juli Slattery points out the source of our longing in her book *Sex and the Single Girl*:

> *Underneath your sexuality is the drive and desire to be*
> *known and loved. God created you as a sexual being*

*so that you might understand what it means to long,
to desire, and to crave intimate oneness. Your sexuality
was never meant to be an isolated physiological urge
that is expressed apart from the rest of who you are as
a woman. You have longings to share your heart, soul,
and body with another person because God made you a
deeply relational and spiritual woman.
Your greatest need for intimacy however
is to know the God who created you.*[1]

We crave intimacy. We desire to be known and loved. God made us sexual people so we'd have something in us pulling us toward intimacy and oneness. We want to share our heart, body, and soul with someone because God made us that way. However, over time we discover that a person cannot fully meet this craving we have. God made us with a need no human could fill so we would look beyond human relationships—so we would look for Him. Because He is perfect and sinless, there is no selfishness in Him to fall short of what we hoped He would be. Knowing God and being known by Him ultimately meets our deepest desire for intimacy.

Intimacy starts with knowledge, so building an intimate relationship with God begins with learning about Him and opening your heart up to Him.

Let me walk you through practically how this all works for me.

I'm an anxious person. My grandmother was a worrier, and it got passed down straight to me. I'm a firstborn, type A perfectionist. You name it, I worry about it. The song "Hakuna Matata" actually bothers me. Take for example, right now. Right now I am experiencing some anxiety over this book—will I get it written and edited to meet my publishing deadline? Have I handled God's Word accurately? Have I represented marriage well? Have I illustrated my points clearly? Have I communicated in a way that connects with women much younger than me? Will they actually read it? Will it help them? Will this story even illustrate my point?

I'm also thinking about all the other things I've neglected to get this chapter done. I need to go to the bank and the post office. There is a stack of bills on my desk. The bathrooms are dirty. There is laundry to be done, weeds to pull. Have I filled out that form for my son? I could go on, but it makes me feel more anxious. I'm not particularly proud of this feature in my life, but it is a day-to-day struggle for me.

But then I come across a verse like this in the Bible:

Give all your worries and cares to God,
for he cares about you.[2]

The Bible says that God cares for me. Because He cares for me, I am told to give my anxiety to Him. The verse even says *all* of my anxiety.

Well, a few things happen when I am reminded of this truth about God:

First of all, I feel special that He cares about me. I mean, He has a bazillion people and things to keep up with, but my anxiety over writing a few paragraphs is something He wants to hear about and deal with? I respond by sharing with Him the things I am anxious about. Because He asks for *all* my anxiety, I feel free to let loose and share everything. I can talk to Him about the things in my life that overwhelm me, and I feel heard and understood. My worries are not too much for Him to handle. I am not too much for Him. I can be fully me, anxious thoughts and all. He sees me, even the not so great parts of me, and He cares for me. I feel known and loved just as I am.

I feel provided for. Not only does He want to hear about my problems, He actually has the power to do something about them. An all-powerful God is going to handle my concerns as I throw them on Him. Talk about making a girl feel taken care of! If God wants to handle my problems, and has the power to do so, I can start to trust Him with the anxieties that are burdening my heart. I begin to unload this heavy sack of worries I am carrying around and "throw" them onto Him. My heart becomes lighter as I trust Him to handle the things I cannot. I can rest in the care of a good God who is big enough to handle me and my troubles.

I feel known. I feel loved. I know more about The One who loves me. He cares about my heart and the things that are important to me. He is big enough to take care of me. I can trust Him.

That's intimacy.

I could share these concerns with my husband, Sean. He also cares about what concerns me. I'm sure if I did, he would hug me and tell me that he loves me. Because he is more laid back about details than I am, he may not relate to or understand my anxieties. He may offer some well-meaning advice about how to view my situation differently, which I would love to do but probably can't because I am too anxious. He may even offer to help with the kids or housework or errands (all of which he has done repeatedly during this writing process), but ultimately he can't take away my anxiety. I'm sure he would if he could, but he doesn't have that power. I have a loving and supportive husband who serves me like crazy and would do anything he could for me, but he cannot completely understand my burdened heart or take my anxieties from me.

Intimacy with God surpasses what I can experience with a man.

However, having intimacy with God actually benefits my marriage. Because my relationship with God meets my deepest needs, I am satisfied. I'm not looking to my man to fulfill needs that are beyond his ability to meet. I am not wanting something from him that he can never give, but instead I can appreciate the ways he tries to know me and love me. Sean, in turn, feels affirmed in his efforts and is able to "win" at being a husband.

The intimacy I experience with God satisfies my deepest needs to be known and loved, freeing my heart to be satisfied with the intimacy I share with my husband.

Because these intimate moments with God usually begin with something I read in the Bible about Him, I actually keep a list of the characteristics of God that I have discovered in the Bible. These are truths about God that I want to remind myself about. I have found that tying them to a letter of the alphabet helps me to recall them later when I need a reminder of who God is (see page 123). Getting to know God and allowing my heart to respond to the truth about Him draws me deeper into intimate relationship with Him, fulfilling the deepest longings of my heart.

He tries to disrupt our intimacy by targeting our view of God.

But even when our hearts are satisfied, we can sometimes hear the sound of a different voice. Whispering doubts. Trying to convince you that God can't fulfill your heart. That He won't give you what you need. That He doesn't see you, is angry at you, could never forgive what you have done.

Where do we get these wrong thoughts about God?

The Bible teaches us that we have an enemy working against us who doesn't want us to know or experience God. He tries to disrupt our intimacy by targeting our view of God. He doesn't have as much power as God, so in order to compensate, he lies. If he can get us to believe a lie, he doesn't need much power. He knows how life-changing it can be when we have an accurate view of God. So guess what? He lies a lot about who God is. He'll try to influence us through anything or anyone he can. It's a method that's proven to be very effective over the years. He's been doing it from day one. Literally.

In the first book of the Bible, we see this same enemy plant doubt in Eve's mind about God's character.[3] God had told the first two people, Adam and Eve, they could eat from the multitude of trees He provided for them, but there was one tree He told them not to eat from. The enemy influenced Eve to believe that God wasn't good, and He was holding out on her. Well, she believed this lie about God, and then she made a choice to disobey one of the few commands God had given them. She influenced her husband as well. As a result, there were big consequences for her, for her marriage, and there are still consequences for us today.

Our enemy hasn't changed much. He will come along and cause you to question God's goodness and plan for you. He's pretty crafty, so it is easy to fall for his lies.

How do I know this? He's used it on me too many times to count.

In college I heard a little voice in my head that said,

"You don't want to follow God and be weird, do you? If you follow God, He'll ruin your life by making you do things you don't want to do. Guys who follow God are weird too. You don't want one of them, do you?" Since I didn't know God well, I fell for it.

Then later, when I was single and did have a relationship with God, I heard this voice: "God is cheating you! You are making choices to follow Him, and you are throwing your life away. Every girl around you is getting married, and you are missing out. God is withholding what's best for you!" My enemy was trying to cause me to doubt God's goodness and plan for my life.

> *I have found that it is crucial to maintain a correct view of God in my mind—both as a single woman and a married one.*

I had to go back and remind myself of who God is and what He has done for me.

As a married woman, the enemy whispers lies to isolate me not only from God but also from my husband. "Sean doesn't really listen to you. If he did, he would understand how you feel." If the enemy can get me to expect the kind of intimacy from my husband that only God can give, it can plant seeds of doubt in my mind about his love for me. Our enemy is cunning and knows the lies that will do the most damage.

I have found that it is crucial to maintain a correct view of God in my mind—both as a single woman and a married one. It helps me see the enemy's lies for what they are and maintain my intimacy with God and my husband.

You know, as wacky as I thought that Sunday school lady was thirty years ago, *I am* now experiencing the intimacy with God she talked about. God *is* my everything. *I am* completely myself with Him, and *I'm not* afraid of rejection. He's my favorite person to be with. I *want to know* all I can about Him and *can't wait* to be face to face with Him someday. I think about Him *all the time*, and in case you haven't noticed, *I can't* stop talking about Him.

If you know God well, you'll learn to love Him.
If you love Him, it's easier to trust Him.
If you trust Him, you're more willing to obey Him.
And, if you obey Him, you'll experience His best.

You can love your husband, before you even have one, by getting to know God and enjoying intimacy with Him, so you won't look to your husband to meet needs only God can.

Key Truth
Whom have I in heaven but you? I desire you more than anything on earth. Psalm 73:25

Points to Ponder
Where do you go to find the intimacy you long for?

Action Step
Read your Bible every day and start learning more about who God is and what He's done for you.

Additional Resources
The God You Can Know, Dan DeHaan
For years this has been one of my favorite books on knowing God.

Unsatisfied, Sean Vollendorf
This is my husband's book. In the latter half of the book, he goes through many of God's attributes in a style only he can. It's my fave.

A–Z Bookmarks, available at www.kimvollendorf.com
This is a simple tool I've developed to keep track of the things I learn about God. Using the alphabet to help organize them allows me to more easily recall them later.

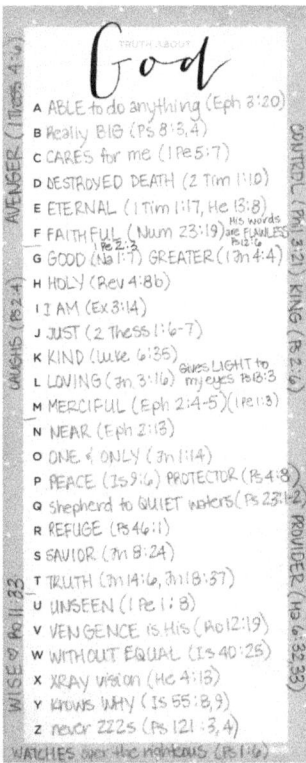

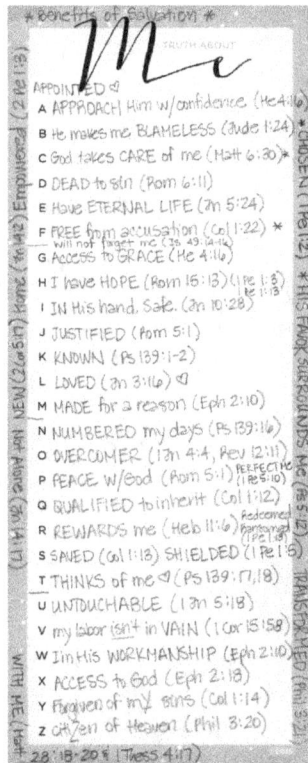

Endnotes

1. Dr. Juli Slattery, *Sex and the Single Girl* (Chicago: Moody Press, 2017), 19.

2. 1 Peter 5:7.

3. Genesis 2–3.

*For me, my freshman year of college was a super confusing time.
I went from being at a high school where I felt known and valued
because of my achievements to being at a college where no one
knew who I was. I desired more than anything to find my worth
in something, and eventually that "something" I was searching
for turned into a hunt for "someone." I started going to parties
and getting drunk so I could "have the courage" to hook up with a
stranger. I knew this wasn't a way to find the type of relationship I
was looking for, but I pushed those thoughts away because it made
me feel desired and loved, at least for a night. I continued to live
like this for a year until eventually it just left me depressed because
I felt so disposable. I struggled with purity because I wanted guys to
like me, and I did whatever it took to make that happen.*
—**Single girl, twenty-one years old**

———————————

*Growing up, no one ever told me why I should avoid sexual sin.
They just said, "Don't have sex." What they weren't telling me is
sexual sin also has emotional consequences, and that one day it
would be so devastating to tell the man you are going to marry your
past history and that you didn't save yourself for him. Even though
Jesus's redemption and grace in our lives allowed us to forgive each
other's pasts and enter marriage with renewed hearts and bodies, I
still wish someone would have told me that your actions and sexual
sin today will have serious consequences later.*
—**Wife, married three years**

———————————

*Years ago I went on an overnight trip with some girlfriends. We had
all been married just a few years and most of us to our high school
and college sweethearts. The late night girl talk turned to sex, and
every woman began to share through tears how crossing physical
boundaries while dating her now husband had ended up hurting
their married sex life. We all believed the lie while we were crossing
those lines that it wouldn't matter because we knew we were going
to marry him. It mattered. Crossing boundaries (even with your
future husband) breaks down trust in a relationship,
and that lack of trust carries into marriage.*
—**Wife, married twenty-three years**

10

Save the Oxytocin!

Fight for Purity

We were alone at his place, and it was really late. We hadn't planned to, but we started kissing. *Wait. What am I doing?* The moment seemed to absorb any rational thought. *We should probably stop.* It didn't take long, however, for kissing to weaken my resolve for purity. My thought process became more and more fuzzy. *What is the big deal about kissing?* I knew that we needed to put on the brakes soon or we might do something we would regret later, but...*Ok, in just a minute.* My mind was slipping into neutral, and I didn't want to think about right or wrong. I was getting swallowed up in the moment.

Then out of nowhere, the craziest thing happened. Of all things, a Bible verse popped into my head.

Now maybe you think about Bible verses all the time when you are kissing someone, but honestly, the Bible was the last thing on my mind. My eyes snapped open. It might as well have been a neon sign. I'm not kidding. It wasn't even a verse I had ever tried to memorize, but there it was. I shut my eyes, but the words were still there. It felt like someone had dumped a bucket of ice water over me, and my mind was clear again.

I was tired of those feelings, but it never seemed like I had the strength to do anything about it.

What in the world was I doing?

I remember distinctly thinking, if we were going to keep kissing I would have to totally ignore this neon warning sign and press ahead past the help God was offering me. In that moment of clarity, I just couldn't do it. I stopped and said, "I need to go home." Thankfully my date was an honorable man and said, "You're right." I grabbed my purse and left.

As I drove home, I felt an overwhelming sense of victory—like I had just won a gold medal or something. I had walked out of a situation I could not have left years earlier, and it felt awesome.

I hadn't always fought for purity in my relationships. Physical intimacy had seemed like the normal way to fully express my feelings toward someone and deepen a relationship. But rather than feeling closer to him afterward, I felt lonely, unfulfilled, and ashamed. I was tired of those feelings, but it never seemed like I had the strength to do anything about it.

Before that night I had been growing in my desire for purity. I had read a book called *Passion and Purity*, and it really challenged me. It's the love story of Jim and Elisabeth Elliot. Their story is amazing on a lot of levels. When they were dating, he gently touched her cheek and that was as physically intimate as they got before they married. I was so blown away! Could a man cherish a woman like that? Could a couple love each other intensely and not have sex before marriage? When I read about the Elliots, I realized *that* was the kind of love story I wanted. I prayed, "God, that's what I want." Despite my past, even though I knew I didn't deserve a relationship like that, I resolved to love myself, love my future husband, honor God with my life, and fight for physical purity.

Walking out of a tempting situation that night and doing the right thing was hard, but it was totally worth it. A surge of confidence filled me as I realized I had strength I hadn't had before. I really was becoming someone new, and God had helped me. My resolve for purity became stronger, and I decided not to get in a situation that tempting again.

Most of us are given a basic birds-and-bees lesson around the time of puberty, perhaps a reminder to "use protection" later in our teen years, and that is about the extent of our training in sex and its role in our life. Even if we were raised to "wait for marriage," we probably are still left wondering if what we were taught is really what we want. For the most part, we are left to find our way in this confusing and messy area of life alone.

I have learned a lot the hard way, and would love to share what I have learned with the hope that it can help as you navigate this area. And, though I am no expert on sex, I may have some credentials I haven't mentioned yet. Were you aware of this research?

A study conducted by the University of Chicago, and considered to be one of the most statistically accurate studies on sexuality available today, determined that the most orgasmic women in the United States are

middle-aged, married, conservative Protestant women.[1]
... Furthermore, those having the most sex were not
singles, but women in monogamous marriages—
and they liked it more than singles.[2]

Basically this study says that married church ladies are having better sex, more often than everyone else. ... *Surprise!*

Never underestimate a church lady.

I know first hand that the only way you'll be able to fight for purity in a sex-crazed culture is for you to believe deep down that God has something better out there for you.

As you may know, I'm married. Just for the record, it's monogamous. I'm also assuming by now that you also know that I'm a spiritual woman. I go to a Protestant church. In most circles, I'm considered conservative. Were you also aware of the fact that I am middle-aged?

Grab a cup of coffee and sit down, girls. We need to talk about sex.

I know first hand that the only way you'll be able to fight for purity in a sex-crazed culture is for you to believe deep down that God has something better out there for you. The normal practices of today's sexual culture promise to empower women and give them freedom and fulfillment, but is that the reality you see? Consider these questions as you think about the culture around you:

Why does a young woman give herself sexually to a guy who doesn't even know her or care about her?

If the sex is so thrilling, why does she often have to get drunk to have the courage for it?

*Why would a young woman keep giving herself over
and over again, even though it eventually leaves her
feeling lonely, unfulfilled, and used?*

*Why would she risk giving the deepest part of herself to
a guy who hasn't committed before God and others to
love and cherish her forever?*

*Why does she feel like she has no other choice,
when she does?*

I want you to have an awesome sex life. I really do! Most young women want this too, but they are preparing for it the wrong way. Many of them are doing things that are hurting themselves and will eventually damage the intimacy they are longing for.

What the church ladies show us is that the most satisfying sex occurs the way God intended it to—within marriage. And the best married sex life comes from pursuing purity before you are married. Dannah Gresh defines purity in her book *What Are You Waiting For?*

*Purity is **not** about **not** having sex.
It's about waiting to have it right.*[3]

With that in mind, I'd like to offer a few insights for you to consider.

Many young women believe that sexual experiences are beneficial for a relationship. They reason, "Isn't it good to get lots of practice?" and "How else will I know if he's the right one?" They may feel it is important to make sure there is sexual chemistry in a relationship before committing to marriage.

Ok, let's talk sexual chemistry. Ever heard of the hormone oxytocin? Your body produces this chemical naturally. A momma's body produces huge amounts of oxytocin when she gives birth and breastfeeds. Know what it does? It makes her fall in love and bond with her baby. And if you haven't noticed, mommas LOVE their babies! If you don't believe me, you aren't following any moms on Instagram.

Well, guess what? Your body also releases oxytocin when you share physical intimacy with someone.

Listen to what Dr. Joe S. McIlhaney, Jr. and Dr. Freda McKissic Bush wrote in their book, *Hooked: New Science on How Casual Sex Is Affecting Our Children*:

> *When two people touch each other in a warm,*
> *meaningful, and intimate way, oxytocin is released into*
> *the woman's brain. The oxytocin then does two things:*
> *increases a woman's desire for more touch*
> *and causes bonding [to the man she's been*
> *in physical contact with].*[4]

They continue:

> *The important thing to recognize is that the desire to*
> *connect is not just an emotional feeling. Bonding is real*
> *and almost like the adhesive effect of glue—*
> *a powerful connection that cannot be undone*
> *without great emotional pain.*[5]

Oxytocin "produces a feeling of trust in a person with whom a female is in close contact."[6] It leaves "warm, fuzzy feelings in its wake."[7] *Psychology Today* says this about oxytocin, "After making love a woman might mistake the oxytocin release for feelings that tell her, "This is 'The One,' my perfect partner. Despite those initial feelings, it does not necessarily mean that the person is trustworthy. The perception you have at the moment is an illusion you create about the person that may or may not fit what happens next."[8] Here's the bottom line:

Oxytocin is a powerful chemical that influences your perception of a person. It's a chemical that makes you fall in love with someone. It makes you bond with them. It's sexual chemistry.

Oxytocin works great in marriage. For example, if you have a rough day with your spouse but then later have sex, the oxytocin released makes you think, "This is my perfect partner." This powerful chemical influences your perception of him and your situation. It helps you overlook flaws so you can make it past the hard times. It's awesome! In healthy marriages, it just keeps getting stronger. It's what gives your marriage staying power when things are difficult.

But this sexual chemistry can actually mess things up if you are getting in sexual practice before marriage. Oxytocin might influence you to fall in love with someone and believe them to be your perfect partner when they aren't. You could actually find yourself believing an "oxytocin illusion" about someone rather than evaluating them based on who they truly are. The "love and trust" hormone does its work to help you overlook negative character and faults because that's what it is *supposed* to do!

I bet you all could give examples of this. You've known that girl who keeps going back to a guy who everyone knows isn't good for her. People around her are wondering,

Why does she keep going back to him? She believes she "loves" him. There's chemistry at work—the "oxytocin illusion."

You could even get attached to a guy you don't want to be attached to. He'll get in your head. I recently heard a story about a young woman who had sex with a loser guy and then it ended. Later she found a really nice boyfriend but ended up cheating on him with the loser guy because she had such a strong attachment to the loser guy after sleeping with him. Sexual chemistry can be a powerful force—even if it's pulling you in the wrong direction.

Oxytocin may cause you to fall in love with and end up marrying someone you would never have married if this sexual chemistry had not been there. You could easily end up with a guy who isn't the best for you.

You know, I have a lot of married friends. We talk a lot. Not one of them has ever said to me, "Man, I just don't have sexual chemistry with my husband. We should have slept together before we got married." It has *never* happened.

I have, on the other hand, had married women say to me, "My husband and I are not getting along at all. He's not who I thought I married. What was I thinking?"

If you want to have an enjoyable and lasting marriage someday but are choosing to have sex now, the question you need to answer is this one:

How in the world are you going to know
if he's the wrong guy?

Some girls scoff and say, "Whatever. It doesn't affect me like that. I can love 'em and leave 'em. No problem." If you have developed this pattern, you may have damaged the very bonding mechanism that's there to help you have an enjoyable and lasting marriage someday. If that's you, girlfriend, you need your oxytocin! I'd recommend that you stop engaging in sexual activity and let that mechanism heal. Establish some new patterns of relating to guys. You'll live. I promise. When the time comes to give yourself fully to another person "until death do you part," you will want, for your sake and his, to be whole in your ability to bond with him.

When the Bible says a man and woman become "one flesh" after having sex, God wasn't joking.[9] He designed our bodies to bond. Sexual chemistry is a real and powerful force, and you will be safely and happily under its influence when it is bonding you to your husband.

Now to the other question young women often ask: "Isn't it good to have some sexual practice before marriage?"

To answer that one, we need to talk about self-control.

Self-control is the ability to say no to something you really want, because you know it isn't good for you right now. Self-control is a character quality that is developed over time. It doesn't just appear naturally. It's like a muscle. I may go to the gym and *want* to bench press seventy-five pounds, but if I haven't done the reps to build up to that, it's not going to happen—even if I want to!

Guys who want to have a little "fun" might tell a girl, "Baby, you look so good, I just can't control myself." This compliment may make her feel pretty and desirable so she hooks up with him. If their relationship continues, she reasons it's because she looks so good that he doesn't have self-control with her. She assures herself that he'll totally have self-control when it comes to saying "no" to other girls. When in reality, the guy just told her that he doesn't have self-control around good-looking women.

This is important. Please listen:

Self-control doesn't develop walking down an aisle
or putting on a wedding band.

There are a lot of temptations out there that tear relationships and marriages apart. Strong self-control muscles are needed to fight off these temptations. If you are in a relationship without a self-control muscle, a wedding won't magically produce what is needed to start and sustain a trust-filled marriage. Even if purity has not been a priority in your relationship up till now, it is not too late to set some standards together and start working as a team to build self-control before marriage.

Getting married is the starting line for sex, not the finish line. That's the fun part! You don't need practice or skill beforehand. You'll make a lot of fun memories getting it figured out. The best part is that you won't have to worry about giving yourself only to be rejected. And you bring trust into your marriage bed, which is the foundation of the intimacy you crave.

If you are not choosing self-control in your relationship now, the question you need to answer is this one:

How will you know if he will have self-control later
when he is in tempting situations with other women?
How will you know if you will have self-control as well?

Now hear me out, I've been around young women long enough to know what most are doing. I haven't always been a follower of Christ, and I haven't always pursued sexual purity in my own life. I've certainly made some mistakes. I have accepted the forgiveness God offered me and the consequences that came, and I kept moving forward. I want you to understand how the choices you make now will affect you and your future relationships. Understanding how sexual intimacy is designed to work will empower you to make choices now that will help you. My story has a happy ending. It wasn't too late for me to make a change to fight for purity, and it's not too late for you either.

I also know many of you have had sexual things forced on you that you didn't want. You'll have to deal with the consequences of someone else's sins, and it stinks. My heart hurts that you have had to go through that. God is just, and He has a way of paying back those who use others sexually.[10] He has a proven history of stepping into hurts like that and turning things around for the better. You are not alone. There are many women who have amazing marriages even though they have sexual hurt in their past. It will be important for you to resolve these things, and I'll provide some resources at the back of the chapter. It's not too late for you to fight for purity either.

But I was convinced that God had something better out there for me, and I held on and kept fighting.

Was it easy to fight for purity? No. It was hard. Did I always want to fight for purity? No. There were days that I didn't want to. Did people make fun of me? Yes, they did. Did I wonder if there were any guys out there who wanted purity? Of course. Was I scared that none of them would want a girl like me? Yes! But I was convinced that God had something better out there for me, and I held on and kept fighting.

Sean and I didn't know each other at the time, but he started pursuing purity in college too. When we dated we made purity a priority. We talked through our standards and had people ask us about them. We didn't lay on the couch together to watch movies, and we weren't staying up talking to each other until 2:00 a.m. We had most of our dates in public places, and when we were alone we opened up curtains and doors. We never even sat on each other's beds.

This may freak you out, but we didn't even kiss while we were dating. As I shared at the beginning of the chapter, I knew kissing could weaken my resolve. I was afraid if Sean Vollendorf kissed me, I'd be a goner for sure. We wanted to honor God and do things right, but we knew our weaknesses, so our first kiss was on our wedding day. I'm not saying you have to do it that way. I am just telling you what worked for us. We fought hard for purity.

Don't get me wrong. If you're thinking Sean and I must be weird and not have the sex drives that you guys experience, then you misunderstand. We intentionally had a short engagement and planned a super-fast wedding. We probably even left our wedding reception earlier than we should have. Trust me, after that many years of singleness, I was done waiting! We worked hard to save everything for our wedding night. *Everything.* It wasn't easy, but we did it, and it was worth it.

What if God's restrictions are actually in our best interests? What if He gave us guidelines to protect us and provide the very best for us? What if those who are trying to follow His way actually get to experience sex in its fullest sense?

Speaking as a representative of the church ladies, I definitely think so.

You can love your husband, before you even have one, by fighting for purity.

Key Truth

Marriage should be honored by all, and the marriage bed kept pure. Hebrews 13:4a (NIV)

Points to Ponder

Why in the world would "church ladies" be having better sex, more often than everyone else? Have you ever considered the idea that God's commands for sexual purity were given for your good?

Action Step

Start saving your oxytocin for your husband.

Additional Resources

These books were not available when I was younger, but I wish they would have been. The women listed below need to become your best friends in this journey of purity. Their books will really help you.

Sex and the Single Girl, Dr. Juli Slattery

Sex and the Single Christian Girl, Marian Jordan Ellis

What Are You Waiting For? The One Thing No One Ever Tells You About Sex, Dannah Gresh

Every Young Woman's Battle, Shannon Ethridge and Stephen Arterburn

For those who have experienced any unwanted sexual activity:

The Wounded Heart, Dan Allender

Door of Hope, Jan Frank

In some cases, professional counseling may be needed, but these books can get you started off in the right direction.

For all things related to sex and sexuality:

www.authenticintimacy.com

This is Dr. Juli Slattery's website and through her podcasts, webinars, and books, she pretty much covers it all.

Purity Advice

Suggestions from other young women who are fighting for purity:

"I think that your motives for wanting to be pure can help you remain in victory. If your only reason for purity is to follow a set of rules or to be pure for your husband then you may not stick with it. Or if you do, you will not experience the full satisfaction of remaining pure out of obedience to God."

"For a long time I never thought I was good enough to have a relationship with God because I had messed up so much in the past. Pursuing purity to me was like uncovering the truth of God...no matter what my past was, He wanted to love me and show me that he loved me. Purity was my way of responding back to God's love for me. If He died on the cross to show me He loved me, then I wanted to live a life according to His standards to show Him I loved Him back. It wasn't easy, but it's definitely been worth it. I've learned so much more about God's love for me now."

"Have a good community of girls who are pursuing purity alongside you! Trying to be pure is hard in a world that promotes sex, but people to keep you accountable and encourage you in this journey makes it so much easier!"

"I always try to go to the talks on relationships at our campus ministry and church, because I think that it is wise to constantly be reminded of the value of purity and ways to become and stay pure."

"When my boyfriend and I started pursuing purity, we had already crossed a lot of boundaries. We had to back the line way up to not even kissing in order to avoid the temptation to fall back into old patterns."

"Sin always grows in darkness, so until we confess areas of sin to God and other people, it will continue to grow—you won't be able to just get rid of it or handle it on your own."

"One of the hardest things for me was admitting that the relationship I was in for four years was actually hindering me from going deeper with God. Our relationship was full of old sin patterns, and in the end I had to be real with myself that his views of pursuing purity and God weren't the same as mine. I knew I needed to choose between him and God. I thought it was something I could never do, but for the first time in my life I decided to trust that God had my best interest in mind and wanted to give me more than I could imagine if I would simply trust Him and His plan to bring me a healthy relationship and marriage."

"We need to change our view of sexual purity from 'rules you have to follow if you're a Christian' to viewing purity as a path God has shown that leads to incredible marriages (and saves us a lot of hurt). I also think that it is important to remember that purity is attainable for everyone, even those who have messed up."

"It's hard in college, but I don't go into guys' rooms. I try to hang out with guys mostly in public places. Being in a room where the only place to sit is a bed just feels too intimate."

"I used to be embarrassed to talk about these issues with other Christian girls because I felt like they would think less of me or think of me differently; however, when I started opening up about the things I struggle with, these friends only loved me more because they wanted to help me."

"Scripture memory has been crucial in the battle. It's hard to get knocked around by what the world is saying when you are rooted in what God's Word says about purity."

"I think the most helpful thing for me was trusting older women in my life to help me, not judge me, and keep me accountable. It was a hard thing to be vulnerable about, but once I was, it helped me to forgive myself and it helped me to fight temptation. Being fully known by people was helpful for me in fighting for purity."

Endnotes

1. Dannah Gresh, *What Are You Waiting For?* (Colorado Springs, CO: Waterbrook, 2011), 155–156.

2. Robert T. Michael et al., *Sex in America: A Definitive Survey* (Boston: Warner Books, 1994), 127–131.

3. Gresh, 93.

4. Joe S. McIlhaney, Jr., MD and Freda McKissic Bush, MD, *Hooked: New Science on How Casual Sex Is Affecting Our Children* (Chicago: Northfield Publishing, 2008), 37.

5. McIlhaney and McKissic Bush, 37.

6. McIlhaney and McKissic Bush, 38.

7. Jennifer Bleyer and Christopher Badcock, Phd, "Tend and Defend," *Psychology Today*, March 7, 2017, https://www.psychologytoday.com/articles/201703/tend-and-defend.

8. Rita Watson, "7 Tips for Embracing Love While Keeping Oxytocin in Check," *Psychology Today*, February 16, 2017, https://www.psychologytoday.com/blog/love-and-gratitude/201702/7-tips-embracing-love-while-keeping-oxytocin-in-check.

9. Genesis 2:24; 1 Corinthians 6:15–16.

10. 1 Thessalonians 4:6.

I'm so glad that I started to pray for certain characteristics in the man I would one day hopefully marry. When I first heard about the idea, I thought it sounded silly. Years later, I'm getting to marry a man who has all the qualities I prayed for and more! It helped me to know my standards and not compromise on what I wanted in a husband.

—Val, twenty-four, engaged

———————

I longed for a relationship, but didn't see any guys around me that matched my standards and were following God. I started writing in a journal about qualities I wanted in a husband, specific prayers for him, and quotes I found along the way. The night before our wedding I gave him the journal, and it was so special for both of us to see my prayers unite with the amazing man God had brought me.

—Molly, thirty-three, married ten years

11

Ask Him for him

Pray for Him

During my junior year, I went on a church retreat for college students. At this retreat they offered workshops you could pick and choose to attend. In one of the workshops I chose, the lady leading it happened to mention that she prayed for her husband when she was single. I was new to following God, and I had never thought of that before. My big takeaway from the entire weekend was that I wanted to start praying for my future husband. On the bus ride home, I remember looking out the window and saying a prayer for my future husband for the first time ever. It was the fall of 1985.

In the fall of 1985, my future husband was just about to turn thirteen. He didn't believe in God. He didn't go to church. In fact, he didn't really know anyone who was following God at that time. It wasn't even on his radar. Well, a few months after I started praying for him, Sean met the guy who would later lead him into a personal relationship with Christ.

Was it just a coincidence?

Over the years I continued to ask God for a husband. I poured out my heart to Him about wanting to be married someday. I asked God to bring the right man at the right time. I kept a list of things I prayed for, and I would jot them down as they came to mind. I prayed mainly for character qualities and spiritual development. I chose not to pray every day for him because I didn't want my heart to be all tied up emotionally thinking about a husband all the time when God hadn't given me one. So I chose Tuesdays as the day I would pray that God would bring me a husband. On Wednesdays, I prayed for my future, hoped-for children.

I actually found one of my lists, and these were some of the things I prayed for.

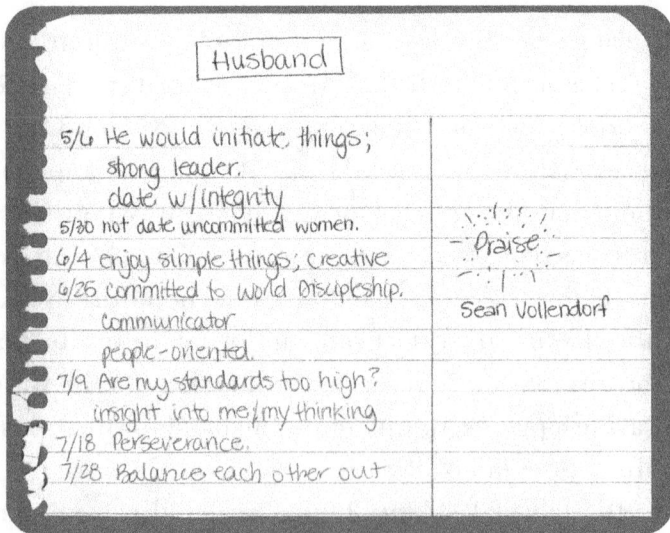

If you knew my husband, you would say these qualities describe him quite well. In fact, it is somewhat uncanny.

Is that just a coincidence?

I'm very aware that trying to do relationships God's way may seem a bit crazy. God wants us to *do* things others *aren't* doing. Then we *aren't* supposed to do things others *are* doing. We start living this somewhat strange life in the midst of those around us. Some of the choices I'm encouraging you to make while you are single might make you question, "Are there even guys *out there* like this?" "How in the world am I going to find a guy like *that?*" I wondered the same things.

The cool thing about being a believer in Christ is that we have access to supernatural help!

The cool thing about being a believer in Christ is that we have access to supernatural help! We have the privilege of asking an all-powerful God to help do what seems impossible, and He has a way of stepping in and making things happen in ways we couldn't even imagine. I've seen God answer my prayers and the prayers of others by providing the kind of man we weren't sure even existed.

You've already heard a lot of my story, but here are some more details of how Sean and I actually met. I was working in an office as a project manager for a campus ministry. I wanted to go off and reach the world for Christ, but I'd pursued a few work options overseas and felt God had shut those doors. As an introvert, gifted at shuffling papers and organizing details, I sat behind a desk in small town America and served others who were overseas. While I was organizing the details for one of the summer programs also under my administrative care, I had to coordinate some details with a young, humorous, outgoing student leader named Sean. After getting off the phone with him one day I thought, "Man, why can't men my age be more like him?"

We'd see each other at various events, but because of our age difference, I didn't really see him as more than a friend. Then, a few years later, Sean asked me to have dinner with him, and you know what happened after that.

Molly is a friend of mine who grew up in Colorado as a daughter of wealthy ranchers. She became the first believer in her family when her dance teacher led her to Christ in middle school. As Molly matured, she noticed most of the relationships around her were unhappy, and she longed for something different. She continued to grow in her relationship with Christ, even though there weren't many guys around her following God. Rather than date an unbeliever, she decided she'd just be single and wait. In college, things didn't change much, and she found herself the single girl living among three roommates with boyfriends.

She wanted to be married, but with no qualified prospects in sight, she continued to pray that God would bring her a husband. As she waited, she started a journal to pray for him. It helped her wait and be content, believing that there was a real person out there she was praying for.

After she graduated, she moved back home for the summer. Friends and family told her, "If you want to get married, you need to put yourself out there." She didn't want to "work it" to try to get a husband. She prayed, "God, I'll know when you bring him to me."

That summer their ranch hired some help from one of the Christian leadership programs being held in the area. Jason, her husband, was one of the guys they hired, and that's how they met. God literally brought him to her doorstep.

Then there was Kristy, a sister of one of my friends. God had given her a heart for missions, so she left Texas and went to live in a small village in Asia. It was so remote, she had to take a train into a neighboring city just to go see the other people on her team. I remember admiring her commitment but also thinking, "Poor girl, there's no way she'll ever get married."

Behind the scenes, Kristy prayed about her need for affection. She wrote out a prayer, "God, I trust You will meet that need." She knew that only God could meet the deepest needs she had. It was a huge desire to get married, but she was determined to only marry a man who was called to missions and wanted to live his life for the gospel.

Well, one day a traveling group of Christians came through that remote village, and among them was a young photographer from Australia. Long story short, God, even in the remotest of places, brought her a husband—and one with a cool accent! I wouldn't believe it if I hadn't seen it with my own eyes, but I was at their wedding. I was embarrassed that I had doubted God's ability.

Another of my favorites is RJ and Kim's story. Years ago, RJ went to Russia for the summer and met a young man named Sergei, who became a Christian during their time together. They kept in touch through letters after RJ left. The next summer, a young girl named Kim, who didn't know RJ, went to Russia to the same city of two million people. Sergei, who was their interpreter, discovered that Kim was from the same city where RJ lived, and he asked if she would take a letter back for him. After Kim went home, RJ came over to get the letter. The rest is history. They have been happily married for over twenty years now.

When I asked Kim about what was happening behind the scenes during this time, this is what she said,

In all honesty, I don't remember praying a whole lot about what I wanted in a mate. I remember having

*ideas about what I wanted and just being consumed
with WANTING to be married, but I don't remember
praying specifically. However, RJ did! He was
twenty-seven when his roommate asked if he was
getting concerned about finding a spouse. He honestly
hadn't thought much about it, being focused on the
responsibilities of a new job in sales.*

*He then remembered one of his [spiritual] leaders
encouraging him to make a list of the things he desired
in a mate. He got down on his knees by his bed that
night with a scratchpad and prayed through some
needs and desires, making a list of both internal and
external characteristics. He then felt challenged that if
he met that kind of girl, he wasn't sure he was the kind
of guy she would [be looking for], so he made
another list of things he desired to become
to be a godly husband for her.*

She continued,

*I've been in awe of [God] to realize that what I might
have wanted wouldn't have been what I needed to
balance me, and wouldn't have been best in light
of what the Lord knew life would bring. God gave
me such a humble and attentive husband, one who
unselfishly loves and continually pursues me. One who
creates the fun and spontaneity that makes our family
life so rich and full. I have cautioned my [daughters]
about creating expectations of their own desires,
and have encouraged them rather
to submit their hearts/desires to the Lord,
ultimately asking the Lord to give them what HE
knows is best.*

Most recently, a younger friend of mine, Megan, came home for a brief visit from living overseas. She had been living there for a few years and was getting older than most of the available bachelors she was around. She was only home for a short time, and during her visit she met with her pastor in a coffee shop to fill him in on how the past few years had been. She was unaware that there was a young man at a table near them who could overhear them talking. At a break in the conversation, this young man came up to her and asked, "Have we met?" They hadn't met, but he later became her husband. He was even better than she was hoping for.

While there is no magic formula to pray to get a husband, you can be honest about your desires and take those desires to God in prayer.

Five years earlier, Megan had started a journal to pray for her husband. But she didn't see God answer her prayers, so in frustration she put it away. A few years later, she began to trust that God is good even if He didn't give her a husband. So she picked up the journal again. In faith, she began to pray more specifically about what she desired in man. "Praying for him and journaling about it helped me take the focus off of me and onto the Lord," she said.

Later, after she saw who God provided, she told me, "It's so good to wait and let God blow you away. Why did I even worry about other guys?"

Four different women desiring to get married. Four different stories about how we trusted God for a husband. Two of us prayed for specific, multiple characteristics. One only prayed for a few, and one didn't pray for specific qualities—but her husband did! One kept a consistent prayer journal to pray for a husband, one wrote in it every now and then, one didn't use one at all, and I only prayed on Tuesdays.

So there you go.

What could you take away from these stories? Although they are different, a theme runs through all of them—God is able to bring a husband, even when it looks impossible. While there is no magic formula to pray to get a husband, you can be honest about your desires and take those desires to God in prayer.

Prayer is pretty awesome. If you are in Christ, God's Word says that you have access to God.

I knew that God had never promised me a husband, but one day it hit me that He had never promised that I would be single forever either.

Because of Christ and our faith in him, we can now come boldly and confidently into God's presence.[1]

So let us come boldly to the throne of our gracious God. There we will receive his mercy, and we will find grace to help us when we need it most.[2]

I mean, how awesome is that?

You know what, I choose to take God at His word. I feel the freedom to ask God for things I think I need or want—like help, mercy, grace...and a husband.

Over the years, I've been able to get to know God pretty well. I know that no one loves me more than He does, and He has my best interests at heart. That said, sometimes He answers my prayers, "Yes." Sometimes He answers my prayers, "No." Sometimes He says, "It isn't the right time yet...wait." Whatever the answer, I can trust Him.

When I was single and was struggling through God's plan for me, I knew that God had never promised me a husband, but one day it hit me that He had never promised that I would be single forever either. He *had* promised, however, if I put Him first and lived as He taught, that He would meet my needs.[3] I had needs for companionship, sexual intimacy, and I desired a partner to work alongside for God's kingdom. I decided to take my needs to God and pray for them.

I like the way Candice Watters said it in her book, *Get Married*:

Like good food satisfies an empty belly, for most believers, good marriages satisfy loneliness and other core needs. God's command to be fruitful and multiply and take dominion of the earth persists. The work He called us to is not yet complete. The assignments of the garden still stand. And marriage is central to that work. Unless your calling would be inhibited by marriage and family, and you're especially gifted to surrender marriage and all its benefits for lifelong celibacy, marriage is still normative and the appropriate channel for your God-given desires for companionship, sexual intimacy, and the partnership essential for completing your life's work while bringing God glory.[4]

I know some incredible single women who aren't married yet. God has not brought them a husband, and they would really like to get married. It doesn't make sense to me, so I pray on their behalf and look forward to seeing what God will do. In the meantime, they are not waiting around. They are content with where God has them, and they trust He knows best.

God's plan is different for each one of us, but I do know

God said that it was "not good for the man to be alone."[5] He also told Adam and Eve to "be fruitful and increase in number."[6] Marriage seems to be a necessary ingredient for each of these.

Learning to place my needs and wants in God's hands through prayer has been something that has carried into my marriage.

Because of that, I totally think it's OK to want to get married and to ask God for a husband.

I'm going to trust His decision either way, but I feel the freedom to humbly ask God for what I think I need or want. God is not a genie in a lamp, but as my Father, I can approach Him and ask. I don't want to be guilty of not believing that He is able to do something or not even asking Him about it. Beth Moore has a great quote that I often refer to.

We can always hope and pray diligently for a miracle. If, in God's Sovereignty, He chooses to accomplish His purposes another way, let it not be that we have not because we asked not (James 4:2) or that we have not because we believed not (Matthew 9:29).[7]

When we see God answer our prayers, it grows our faith. Maybe you don't believe praying about something changes things. Maybe it's because you have never seen God answer specific prayers, or maybe you just think these things are coincidence. I've only shared with you a couple of the instances where I believe with all my heart that God chose to do the impossible as an answer to prayer. There are so many more. Prayer works.

Learning to place my needs and wants in God's hands through prayer has been something that has carried into my marriage. I continue to pray for Sean, but now I pray for him every day, not just on Tuesdays. Sean and I regularly pray together. We pray for our marriage, our kids, our work, our needs, and our wants. It ties our hearts together in a special way, and we get to see God do some miraculous things on our behalf.

And it all started on the bus ride home from the fall retreat. I'm really glad that the workshop leader mentioned it, so I'm gladly passing that advice on to you.

You can love your husband, before you even have one, by praying for him.

Key Truth
Don't worry about anything; instead, pray about everything. Tell God what you need, and thank him for all he has done. Philippians 4:6

Points to Ponder
Is there anything keeping you from asking God for what you think you need?

Action Step
If you want to get married, start praying for a husband. Ask that God would bring the right man at the right time in the right way. Also pray that you'll become the type of woman the man you're praying for would be praying for.

Endnotes

1. Ephesians 3:12.

2. Hebrews 4:16.

3. Matthew 6:33.

4. Candice Watters, *Get Married: What Women Can Do to Help It Happen*, (Chicago: Moody Publishers, 2008), 28.

5. Genesis 2:18.

6. Genesis 1:28 (NIV).

7. Beth Moore, *Believing God*, Goodreads.com, https://www.goodreads.com/work/quotes/1008529-believing-god.

I remember playing games like M.A.S.H. growing up, and I would daydream about my future husband and the house we would live in. Nowadays it's just a win to take care of the small bedroom and bathroom I live in right out of college. I'm excited to use my single years as a time to grow my hospitality skills, so that one day if I do get married, I'll be a little bit more prepared to care for those who come into my home!"

—Hallie, twenty-three years old

———————————

One day I woke up and I realized I hadn't hung a single thing on my walls. I was waiting. I was waiting for marriage to create a dream home; a home that was restorative, a home that I and others could retreat to, to find rest. That same day I decided I wouldn't wait anymore, that I'd love and embrace where God had me. So I hung picture frames, moved around furniture, and began creating a place people could feel loved, cared for, and at home. It was the best compliment when friends would come and go and tell me how cozy, and peaceful my apartment was. It felt like home to them too.

—Alyssa, twenty-six years old

———————————

I have always enjoyed cooking and hosting others in our home. Now that I have kids, I've come to realize hosting isn't all about my perfect meal or spotless house. It's about inviting others into my life and letting them be part of my family— both the sweet toddler mealtime prayers AND the highchair tantrums.

—Brooke, married six years

12

Home Sweet Home

Create a Home

When I was single I looked forward to having a wedding shower someday. How fun it would be to have friends and family bless you with wonderful new things to make a home! As the years went by and no man came, there was no shower. My home was always an eclectic assortment of what my parents passed on and what my roommates and I could pool together. I hit the jackpot, however, when Jill moved in.

Jill was an interior design major. She didn't have lots of money or fancy things either, but she transformed our simple little apartment into a cozy, appealing home that we were proud of. She took some old wooden patio furniture, painted it and stuffed her own cushions for the chairs. With her dad's help, she built our bookcase and our coffee table. She took the base of a birdbath (which weighed a ton by the way), secured a piece of circular cut wood on the top, and then sprayed it with speckle paint to make it look like granite. Jill was Pinterest embodied before Pinterest was even a thing.

Jill taught me about the importance of creating warm home ambience—lighting from lamps, fragrance from a candle, playing background music. Jill knew how to take the items she had available to create an environment that made people feel welcome.

Jill showed me how to make a home, even when I didn't have a husband.

While we were roommates, we decided to take turns cooking dinner for each other during the week. These dinners turned out to be some of my favorite memories of this season of my life. At the time I was a macaroni-and-cheese girl, but Jill would do "gourmet" things like broil fish in the oven. I remember once she opened a can of peaches, topped them with little sprinkles, and then announced "Fiesta Peaches!" when she set them on the table. She was all about creativity and presentation in the kitchen. Man, she was fun to live with!

We may not have had all the bells and whistles in our kitchen, but we had what it took to make macaroni and cheese, broil fish, and open a can of peaches. We'd light a candle, play some music, and laugh over a nice dinner. Jill showed me how to make a home, even when I didn't have a husband.

I was sad when Jill moved out to get married, and I was not surprised when she later launched a successful design business.[1] I stayed single a few more years, and each time I moved to a new place, I always sought out a design-savvy friend in town to help me get my house set up. Some people just naturally have the gift, and my sister was the one who ended up with all those genes in our family.

I tried to keep the tradition of roommate dinners going, and when some of my new roommates had conflicting schedules and couldn't eat dinner together regularly, I started recruiting other friends.

Leigha was a friend who took me up on that offer, and we took turns cooking dinner for each other at our respective apartments each Wednesday. It was so fun to try out new recipes together. We had some wins and some losses—my overly salted attempt at my grandmother's purple hull peas was a definite fail, and her parmesan chicken was an undisputed winner. Acting as each other's cooking guinea pigs forged a fun friendship between us.

Inviting others into our homes can make them feel loved and cared for.

Home can be such a wonderful place. At home we can experience comfort and safety and peace from the outside world. It's amazing what can happen over a single act of hospitality. We can't control the world beyond our doors, but we can make choices about what it's like inside our doors. Perhaps some of you have grown up in a home that was not a peaceful place. When you move out, you have the opportunity to create something different for yourself.

Home, of course, is more than furniture or food or candles—it's about loving those around you. Inviting others into our homes can make them feel loved and cared for. Hospitality begins now with what you have. It doesn't have to wait until you get married.

Nancy DeMoss Wolgemuth, who married for the first time when she was fifty-seven, said this on her website at ReviveOurHearts.com:

At the heart of the gospel, at the heart of the cross is the Lord Jesus opening His heart and His arms wide and saying to sinful men and women, "I want you to come home with Me. I want to make a home for you." And so when we put God's priorities on our homes, we're following the example of our homemaker heavenly Father, our homemaker Savior. Our goal is to create for our husband, our children, our neighbors, our roommates, our guests a taste for our ultimate home in heaven.[2]

Once, with three little boys in tow, I had to drop off something to my single friend, Erin. As soon as we all walked in her door, she pulled out a little basket of toys for my boys. I had never seen anything like it! Erin, as a single woman without children, knew about hospitality, and she was ready for even her youngest guests to feel at home in her apartment. Erin continues to show hospitality, now making a happy and inviting home with her husband and two kids.

Creating a place of welcome can truly be a delightful opportunity. If you ever get around my friend Amy, she'll make you see the kitchen as a wonderland, full of opportunities to "Love. Welcome. Serve." She's the owner of the cutest boutique kitchen store, has her own cooking show on TV, and just published a cookbook.[3] She even shared one of her go-to soup recipes with us (see page 165)! I always get inspired to love on people by cooking for them when I am around her.

To be honest, similar to decorating, cooking has never naturally been my thing. I like to eat good food, but I don't instinctively thrive in the kitchen. But I do love my family, and the fact is that we need to eat. Eating out all the time is not an option for us, and eating cereal for dinner gets old. Because my schedule is the most flexible, I do most of the cooking in our home.

Often my middle son, Simeon, will step in and cook. He naturally enjoys food and cooking. In fact, when he was in elementary school, he'd pack a salad with a dressing he made all by himself in his school lunch. I mean, what kid decides to *make his own dressing?* He likes developing flavors in food, and he enjoys cooking for people. Even as a little guy, he wanted to help cook and serve food. I have a memory of him flipping pancakes when he could barely reach the griddle. When we have people over, he regularly helps with the cooking and entertaining. He's incredible!

People feel loved when you feed them.

I live with all males of varying ages and personalities, and they all love to eat! There is nothing that says "I love you" to my crew like coming home to the smell of dinner cooking. My oldest son, Fisher, told me not long ago as he scarfed down some muffins I made, "Mom, my love language is food!"

People feel loved when you feed them. Cooking has almost become a lost art these days. Feeding others doesn't have to be fancy. For most of our family life Sean has had to work on Sunday nights, so I decided that would be a good night to just have breakfast for dinner. Years ago we started having Belgian waffles for dinner every Sunday night. Waffles are really cheap and a fun way to feed people. We have served a lot of Sunday night waffles. If you are inspired, I'm including my waffle recipe in this chapter (see page 166). You can get a waffle iron on Amazon for around twenty dollars, and they last forever. I have had the same waffle iron for twenty years.

It takes skill and practice to maintain the needs of a home—grocery shopping, laundry, budgeting, mainte-nance, and cleaning. Anyone who has a place to live can make a home, not just married women. These are skills you will need to thrive on your own too—unless you are able to eat out all the time and can hire a cleaning lady.

Home organization is an area I naturally thrive in. I enjoy discovering efficient ways of keeping things in order and having a house that is ready for whatever. It's been a challenge for me to pass off many of the responsibilities to our kids as they get older.

Even though I might be able to do them better, they need to learn those responsibilities for when they are on their own someday. My boys have been doing their own laundry since they were ten. They mow, handle the trash and recycling, and clean their own rooms and bathrooms. They even cook many of their own meals. Skills take practice.

Nancy DeMoss Wolgemuth adds,

> *There is no one-size-fits-all, cookie-cutter approach to how this works. Having a heart for home, being a keeper of your home, will look different for different women—depending on the configuration and the particular circumstances of your family and what best serves their needs at any given time.*[4]

I love on my husband and children by trying to make sure their needs are met first, but I try to manage my home in such a way that I am also freed up to love on those beyond my home. As my boys become more independent, I am freed up to do more. I couldn't have written this book a few years ago, but Sean and I felt the timing was good now. He's had to shoulder many of the home responsibilities for me to pull this off, and he's managed it joyfully.

One Saturday morning, Sean invited a student over to spend some time with him. They planned to do some work out in the yard, and Sean suggested that we all have lunch together. The kids were little then, so I was in full-time mom mode. I'm sure the kids bickered some, and I think I served our guest a simple sandwich for lunch. I can assure you, it was *by far* nothing special. We were just doing normal life. A few days later we received the sweetest note from him. He went on and on about how impressed he was by the way we interacted with each other, what he learned about marriage and parenting, and how loved he felt in our home. I remember reading it and being freshly reminded that a simple, everyday home can be a powerful place to love people.

You can love your husband, before you even have one, by loving your friends and roommates as you learn to make a home.

Key Truth
She carefully watches everything in her household and suffers nothing from laziness. Proverbs 31:27

Points to Ponder
How would your life be different if you practiced hospitality?

Action Step
Make a pot of Amy's taco soup or cook a batch of waffles and invite friends over for dinner. If your living situation doesn't allow you to cook for people, order pizza or pop some popcorn and invite friends over for a game night. Enjoy what happens when you gather people together in your home.

Additional Resources:

www.flylady.net

This is a free online resource. The Fly Lady has helped me with a system for keeping my home clean and clutter-free.

www.emeals.com

I wish this had been available when I was first on my own. It's a great resource for getting started in the kitchen—meal planning, budgeting, and cooking. They have a variety of menus available, and they have an option that feeds just two people.

www.EunaMaes.com

You'll find Amy's food blog, cookbook, and other approachable hospitality recipes here.

I learned of taco soup in my early twenties, and boy am I glad I did! This recipe is so simple—filled with store-bought shortcuts and loads of flavor! It feeds a crowd, makes great leftovers, and freezes beautifully for another day. Over the years, I've tweaked the recipe to make it a bit fancier, adding even more flavor. Fancied Taco Soup has long been my go-to recipe for hospitality! Stretch the recipe to fill more bellies by serving it with corn chips, tortilla chips, crackers, and lots of toppings!
—Amy Hannon, author of the cookbook,
Love Welcome Serve: Recipes that Gather and Give[5]

Fancied Taco Soup
{feeds about 10 people, depending on your people}

1 lb. ground beef

1/2 lb. ground hot breakfast sausage

1 small yellow onion, chopped

1 can black beans

1 can light red kidney beans

1 can cannellini beans or other white beans

1 can Rotel tomatoes with juice {tomatoes with green chiles}

1 small can chopped green chiles

1 1/2 cups frozen whole kernel corn

1 packet of taco seasoning

1 packet of dry Hidden Valley Ranch dressing mix

2 tablespoons tomato paste

1 teaspoon brown sugar

3-5 jalapeno rings, chopped {jarred or fresh} optional

In a big, heavy pot, brown the beef and sausage with the onions. Tilt the pan and scoop out about 3/4 of the grease and discard, keeping a little grease for flavor.

Dump in the cans of beans, Rotel tomatoes, chopped green chiles, corn, seasonings, sugar, and chopped jalapeños. Stir together and add a little water or more to get the liquid how you want it. I like it a little thicker with less liquid. Bring to a boil, reduce to a simmer, adding more water as you need. Allow to simmer for at least 30 minutes, preferably 45–50 minutes to develop flavor. Taste as you go, adding salt and pepper, more liquid, etc. Serve soup with corn chips, crackers, or tortilla chips. Any of these are great to serve as toppings: sliced avocado, chopped tomatoes, black olives, cilantro, green onions, shredded cheese, and sour cream.

Vollendorf Belgian Waffles
{feeds my hungry family plus a few friends}

3 large eggs
3 cups all-purpose flour
3 cups milk
3/4 cup vegetable oil
6 teaspoons baking powder
Butter/Syrup

Plug in the waffle iron and let it preheat.

Beat the eggs in a large bowl with a wire whisk or a hand mixer until they are very bubbly. Mix in remaining ingredients. Pour a little less than 1 cup of batter (or what your waffle iron directions suggest) onto the preheated waffle iron. Check with your waffle iron to see how long it needs to cook. My waffle iron has a light that goes out when it is done, which takes out the guess work. Waffle will be hot so remove it with a fork. You can keep cooked waffles warm on a cookie sheet in an oven at 175 degrees.

I usually store leftover waffles in the fridge in a gallon size plastic bag. They will keep for a few days and heat up great in a toaster oven during the week for a quick and easy breakfast.

Chocolate Chip Cookies
"These cookies are the BEST!"
—My boys (and all their friends)

2/3 cup butter flavored shortening sticks (I use Crisco brand)
1 cup sugar
1 cup packed brown sugar
2 teaspoons vanilla
1 teaspoon baking soda
2/3 cup butter, softened
2 eggs
3 cups all-purpose flour
1 teaspoon salt
2 cups semi-sweet chocolate chips

Preheat oven to 375 degrees. Using a hand mixer, stir together shortening, softened butter, brown sugar, regular sugar, eggs, and vanilla. Once it's mixed well, I stir in the rest of the ingredients, using a big spoon.

On an ungreased cookie sheet, form dough into small balls about two inches apart. Bake for about 8–10 minutes or until slightly golden on the edges. Let the pan cool for a few minutes before removing cookies to a cooling rack.

They store best in an air-tight container, but they don't last long around my house.

Endnotes

1. J Lawrence Design, http://www.jlawrencedesign.com/home.html.

2. Nancy DeMoss Wolgemuth, *Revive Our Hearts*, "God's Beautiful Design for Women, Day 35, " https:// www.reviveourhearts.com/ radio/revive-our-hearts/gods-beautiful-design-women-day-35/.

3. Check out Amy's website, *Euna Mae's*, www.eunamaes.com.

4. Nancy DeMoss Wolgemuth, *Revive Our Hearts*, "God's Beautiful Design for Women, Day 34," https:// www.reviveourhearts.com/radio/ revive-our-hearts/gods-beautiful-design-women-day-34/.

5. Visit www.Eunamaes.com

I waited tables all four years of college. I didn't have any bills and loved having the extra cash to spend at my convenience. I bought whatever I wanted or thought "I needed." This attitude followed me after college. It's been hard to train myself to say no to spending and yes to discipline. I wish I would have instilled these principles as soon as I started waitressing at nineteen years old!
—**Haven, single, twenty-nine**

———————

Our marriage has suffered the most pain over our differing views on money. This is so important! I think it is so vital to warn girls that not only should THEY be good at money, but they should find a guy who is too.
—**Wife, married three years**

13

Adulting

Manage Your Money

I was a trust fund college girl thanks to thoughtful, benevolent relatives. This trust fund, combined with generous parents on an orthodontist's salary, allowed me to pursue my college degree without financial concern. I'm embarrassed to say that I never even knew the balance in my bank account. Money just always seemed to be there for whatever I needed.

As you can imagine, entering the real world after having this kind of financial background would be more than an eye-opener for me. There would be no more trust fund, and I would be on my own financially. Money would stop appearing magically in my bank account. I told myself that surely I would be fine because I had a job. I was going to have a career in campus ministry.

The week before my last set of finals, a festive table

with balloons caught my eye in front of the student union. Back in those days, not all students could get credit cards, and they were wooing graduating seniors to apply for one. The workers behind the table told me it would be good to have my own card for emergencies and for "establishing credit." Well I totally bought in. I felt I was "adulting" well as I walked away from the table with my free t-shirt, water bottle, and newly established line of credit.

"I love you, Kim, but I'm not going to give you a husband to fix this. You have some things to learn about money."

A huge dose of reality was waiting for me.

Placing a credit card in my hands at that time in my life was very smart for the credit card company but somewhat dangerous for me. It didn't take me long to realize that I didn't need a credit card, especially one with an annual fee.

One night in frustration, I finally called the company to cancel it. My roommate, Kristen, cheered me on, but I was not adequately prepared for the well-trained representative who answered my call. Somehow, in a matter of minutes, she had talked me out of canceling it. When I hung up the phone Kristen asked, "What happened? Why didn't you cancel it?" I was embarrassed. I put my head in my hands and sighed, "I really need a husband. I can't even cancel a credit card."

I can imagine at this point God was probably thinking, "I love you, Kim, but I'm not going to give you a husband to fix this. You have some things to learn about money."

The years of singleness that followed had a lot of ups and downs financially. I had a lot to learn, but I hung in there and walked away with very valuable lessons.

One of the first things I learned to do when I was on my own financially was to honor God by giving some of my earnings back to Him each month. In college I started supporting a child through Compassion International, but I wanted to be faithful to give a regular percentage of my monthly income to my church too. I also wanted to support someone working to take the message of God's love to people who hadn't even heard of Jesus. I wasn't able to give a lot, but it really felt good to give something consistently out of the money I earned.

One of my mentors, Carol, taught me about honoring God with the "first fruits" of the money I made.[1] This meant I needed to do my giving first from each paycheck. To be honest, it was hard at times, but I got in the habit of writing checks to my church and the missions I supported first, before I spent money on anything else. It helped me develop a pattern of sitting down at the beginning of the month to get my money in order. Surprisingly, it actually brought a lot of joy.

A few years later, after my parents' divorce, my dad gave me two books on the biblical view of handling money. I wanted desperately to learn from their mistakes, so I read both of them. I started taking steps to put some of the things the books suggested into practice.

It took me a little while, but I slowly developed a written spending plan. I tried to think through all of my expenses— giving, rent, food, clothes, car, entertainment, medical, gifts, and so on—and figured out a budget of how each paycheck would be divided. I tried to set back money each month for the things I might need later, like auto maintenance, medical expenses, and Christmas gifts. I had to learn some discipline to stay in that spending plan, but it felt good to be in control of my money.

I got in over my head a few times with my credit card and finally decided debt was just not for me. I called the credit card company again, and this time I successfully cancelled my card. I eventually just used a credit card for my gas, and I paid it off every month. Debit cards weren't a thing during these days, so I handled everything with checks or cash. I used an envelope system to start saving for things like clothes and vacation. (I put cash in a designated envelope each month as a way of saving for future expenses.) I found that spending money I had set aside ahead of time was way more enjoyable than spending money with a credit card and having to pay the money back later with interest. I felt free to enjoy spending the money I had saved for fun things like clothes or gifts rather than guilty or anxious about buying things I didn't have money for.

My single years allowed me to learn the value of a dollar, and it felt good to handle money well.

As year after year went by without a husband, I figured I needed to start learning about investing for the future. Although I wished I would have started investing earlier, I jumped in and got started. When my mom passed away, she left some money for me, and I was thankful for the lessons I had learned. I decided to use my inheritance to make a down payment on a house. I invited two girls to live with me, and the rent they paid covered the cost of my monthly mortgage.

My single years allowed me to learn the value of a dollar, and it felt good to handle money well. I learned how to do things adults have to do with money like buy insurance and pay taxes. I also appreciated how good it felt to work, to give, and to keep my expenses within my budget.

By the time Sean and I met, I had come a long way from my college days. I was handling my money pretty well. I was a homeowner, and I didn't have any debt other than my house. I lived each month on a budget, saved regularly and spent within my income. When Sean invited me out to Colorado to meet his family over spring break, I pulled out my envelope marked "Vacation" with the money I had saved and said, "This is what I have to spend while I am out there." Sean thanked me for offering to use my vacation fund, but said he wanted to cover my costs for the trip. He was the best!

To be honest, Sean was the best in almost every way possible, but I quickly learned that he didn't know much about money management. It concerned me. I had much more experience in handling money than he did. I realized I was taking a financial risk in our relationship. Sean had shown faithfulness and responsibility to God in every other area of his life, so I had no reason to doubt he would do the same in the area of money management as well. After our engagement, however, it began to weigh heavily on me. I had watched conflicts over money destroy marriages, and I knew good money management was critical.

With uncanny timing, an old friend sent me a brochure from the financial counseling ministry he and his wife had become a part of. He had heard I was engaged, and he offered to take us through their financial counseling services before we got married. It seemed like the perfect solution for us. I asked Sean about it that night when we talked on the phone.

"Hey Babe, you know how I have been a little nervous about money issues? Well, Jeff and Deb sent me a brochure about the financial counseling ministry they are doing now, and they've offered to do some premarital financial counseling with us. Would it be OK if we looked into that? I think it would be really helpful."

He said, "Jeff? As in your *old boyfriend?*" "Well, um yeah," I said.

(Ok, so I had dated some off and on throughout my single years, and Jeff just *happened* to be one of the guys I had dated. *Minor detail.*)

So long story short, a few weeks later there we were — me, Sean, my old boyfriend, and his wife — circled around all of our bank statements spread out on their coffee table. It was very humbling to expose ourselves financially. I admit it was a bit on the awkward side discussing our financial strengths and weaknesses with an old boyfriend. Sean was an incredibly good sport, and he stepped up to both learn and lead in managing our money.

Together over the next few weeks we watched a series of videos on what the Bible said about money. It was helpful to hear this teaching together. It opened up a lot of great conversations about the values we wanted to have as a family in the area of money. We discussed how we thought we should honor God in our giving. We talked through how we would view debt as a couple, and we committed to not go into debt to buy anything except a house.

Conflict over finances is one of the main reasons marriages fall apart.

One of our assignments was to set up our monthly budget. I distinctly remember shedding a few tears as we hammered out the details. For one, my dog's grooming budget went through some cuts. I adopted "Chloe" after my mom died. Chloe was a Bichon Frise, and it cost more to maintain her hair than it did mine. Also, we were putting back such a minimal amount for our vacations each month, I remember thinking tearfully, "We'll never get to go anywhere!" But when all was said and done, every budget item had money designated for it. As our income increased, we knew which areas we needed to beef up first. We walked down the aisle knowing what our monthly budget would be. We were ready to implement it on day one after our honeymoon.

Having an agreed upon budget ahead of time brought a lot of peace into our marriage. As you may know, conflict over finances is one of the main reasons marriages fall apart. Financial issues rank as the number one reason marriages fail according to Divorce.com.

For the most part, it is the lack of open communication about money problems that jeopardizes a marriage more than the financial problems alone. Everyone has financial issues concerning bills, debts, spending and budgets. How a couple deals with those issues can make or break a relationship. [2]

Through our financial counseling we were able to beat conflict over finances to the punch. In the twenty years we've been married, the hardest financial discussions we have had were when we set up our initial budget. Each year we make some tweaks as we need to, but agreeing on a budget, before we were even married, gave us a baseline for good financial communication and unity.

I remember the first summer after we were married we planned to travel to Colorado, which meant driving across country. When we picked up our car after our pre-trip oil change, the technician grimaced and said, "You'll need to replace all four of these tires before you make a trip like that." That's when I grimaced. I had a flashback of the time when I was a single girl, and I had to buy tires. This was before I had learned about budgeting, and I had to cash in savings bonds my grandma had given me as a little girl to cover that cost! But when Sean and I checked our auto savings fund that we had been putting a little money into every month, we had more than enough to cover it. I wrote a check for the new tires and never even felt the expense. Talk about financial peace and marital harmony!

You may not even be aware of them, but you have deeply ingrained views on money. We all do. Most likely your views have been heavily influenced by the family you grew up in. When you have money, what's your natural instinct? Save? Spend? Give? Invest? Which do you do first? Do you tend to avoid thinking about money? Do you obsess over it? Does it make you stressed?

The answers to these questions will impact your future marriage, especially if you and your spouse have different views. When you are single and the only person in charge of your personal finances, it is a great time to establish wise spending, saving, and giving practices. Take a look back at your last month's bank statement to see what you spent and where. Take note of your natural habits with money and start working toward godly money management now.

You can love your husband, before you even have one, by learning how to manage your money as a single woman.

Key Truth
And if you are untrustworthy about worldly wealth, who will trust you with the true riches of heaven? Luke 16:11

Points to Ponder
Would you currently be a financial asset (advantage) or liability (disadvantage) in a marriage?

Action Step
Put into practice one of the money management tips suggested by my friend at Freedom 5:1 (see page 180).

Additional Resources
Total Money Makeover, Dave Ramsey
Your Money Counts, Howard Dayton
The Treasure Principle, Randy Alcorn
Freedom5:One, www.freedom5one.com
Dave Ramsey, www.daveramsey.com
Crown Financial Ministries, www.crown.org

Endnotes
1. "Firstfruits" is from Deuteronomy 26.
2. "Top 10 Reasons Marriages Fail, *Divorce. com*, "http://divorce.com/top-10-reasons-marriages-fail/.

Financial Tips from Freedom5:One

Your financial health begins with knowing where you want to go and doing the work to accomplish your goals. As a single woman, you can make tremendous progress and prepare yourself for a lifetime of success!

Get Educated: Invest a little time and money to growing in your knowledge about finances. Read 3 important books: Dave Ramsey's *Total Money Makeover* for a practical game plan, Howard Dayton's *Your Money Counts* to gain a deeper biblical perspective on the topic, and Randy Alcorn's *Treasure Principle* to cultivate your heart for generosity. Join a Financial Peace University (FPU) group at your local church. This nine week video series will train and motivate you to manage your personal finances wisely.

Get Practical: Create and follow a written Spending Plan. Every single needs a monthly budget for how much you will spend on food, entertainment, clothes, etc. Plan your giving, and don't forget to set back savings for future expenses like car repairs, medical expenses, and vacations.

Get Help: Want to really excel at the top of your class? Consider working with a Financial Coach who will help you develop a personalized Spending Plan. A Financial Coach can help launch you into greater success through personalized direction, encouragement, support, and accountability.

Get Out of Debt: Consider paying off your debt early. Whether it's student loans, car payments, or credit cards, be passionate about paying off debt.

Get in His Business: Want to be happily married someday? Conflict over money is the leading cause of divorce in America. Bring up financial conversations with anyone you date, and share that financial health is important to you. Casually find out if he is managing his money well. Does he have a plan? Does he pay his bills on time? Is he a giver to his church, ministries, and people in need? Is he diligently working toward paying off his student loans and/or credit card debt? Is he saving money for emergencies and retirement? Financial compatibility matters. Get in his business early in the relationship to find out if you are on the same page regarding money.

If I hadn't learned how to value different personalities while living with my friends in college, I would have been in for a rude awakening in my marriage. I always thought my husband and I were very similar, yet we are only a few months into marriage and I've learned more than ever about the ways we are different. Now, instead of getting upset over it, I am able to see how our differences make us stronger and better as a couple.

—**Melina, twenty-three, married four months**

———————————

Differences that come up between two people in marriage have the ability to divide a couple if they are not seen from a greater perspective. If two people were exactly alike they would grow dull and stagnant. Our differences are a blessing that make each individual a better version of themselves, and together we become a more whole image of the character of Christ Himself.

—**Amanda, thirty, married seven years**

———————————

I'm not sure that marriage would work if two people were exactly the same.

—**Scott and Shelly, married thirty years**

14

Anchors and Sails

Appreciate the Differences

"Hey Kim, you about ready?" Kathy asked.

I've had a few friends named "Kathy" over the years, and this Kathy was a friend of mine post-college. We were roommates and leaders at a summer discipleship program, and it was Wednesday—our day off. The other leaders brainstormed how we should spend the free day, and everyone was pumped about going swimming together. Well, everyone but me.

"You know, I think I'm just going to stay back and get some stuff done here," I responded.

Kathy was shocked. "What? You can't work today. It's your day off! The pool will be fun!"

After being around people every day, all week long, hanging out with more people at the pool didn't sound very refreshing. "You guys go and have fun. I'd really like to stay here by myself and get some stuff done."

"What? Kim, stop working! Just come with us and sit in the sun and do nothing." She was perplexed.

Honestly, catching up on some reading and paperwork sounded wonderful. "No really, I would rather stay here. This is relaxing for me."

Finally she gave up and said, "*Okay*, if that's really what you *want*…" She walked away puzzled, and she enjoyed a fun day socializing at the pool. Meanwhile, I enjoyed a peaceful day quietly reading and doing paperwork alone.

As twenty-something single women, Kathy and I were introduced to the fact that people are often really different from us.

As twenty-something single women, Kathy and I were introduced to the fact that people are often really different from us. I am so thankful for my friendship with Kathy, because through our relationship we both began to recognize that differences weren't necessarily wrong; they were just *different*. We eventually grew in our appreciation of these differences, and we gave each other freedom and grace to be who we were. As an extrovert, Kathy is great with people, and I admire her ability to engage in conversation and make people feel special. As an introvert, I'm good with tasks. I can stay laser-focused and keep up with details. The world needs both of us, and typically these opposites attract each other.

Guess what? I married an extrovert.

Going into marriage with an understanding and appreciation of differences has helped minimize potential conflicts with my *very different from me* husband. I am so grateful for the lessons I learned through my friendships when I was single about relating to people different from myself.

Marriage, at its core, is a friendship between a man and woman. Many of the skills you'll need later in marriage, you can build right now in your friendships. If you want to love your husband, before you even have one, it's important to strengthen your friendships now, while you are single, by appreciating the differences people have.

I've shared this with you before, but here is my working definition of marriage:

Marriage is when a selfish, imperfect man and a selfish, imperfect woman who are very different from each other, learn to love and care for one another, and function together as a team.

I mentioned that I am an introvert, and Sean is an extrovert, but that is the tip of the iceberg of our differences.

For starters, Sean grew up ski racing—clad in spandex, flying down mountains at eighty miles an hour. He likes speed. I don't think I've *ever* gone eighty miles an hour, except maybe on a plane.

> *Many of the skills you'll need later in marriage, you can build right now in your friendships.*

I'm always cold. Sean's always hot. Sean loves risk. I love security. Sean's the guy who rides roller coasters with his hands up the whole time, loving life. If you can get me on a roller coaster, I'm the girl, eyes closed, gripping the handle for dear life.

I like having a plan. I've been carrying a day planner around with me since high school. (Yes, I am *that* cool). Of course, Sean is more spontaneous.

When we order food at a restaurant, I always get what I got last time. *Why change a good thing?* Sean frequently makes a spur of the moment decision to try something completely new.

When Sean pulls into a parking spot, he doesn't have to park straight. I am mortified by this.

In his free time, Sean loves to exercise. I prefer taking a nap. Sean recharges around people. I recharge by being alone.

I like inviting a couple of people over for dinner. Sean prefers hosting a crowd.

Sean grew up in Colorado and never locked his doors. I grew up in Little Rock. I always lock my doors.

When Sean gets money, he wants to save or invest it. When I get money, I want to spend it.

As different as we are, we've learned to appreciate our differences, and together we make a pretty good team.

Sean's very direct in communication. I tend to beat around the bush. He embraces conflict. I avoid it like the plague.

I like to board planes when they first announce they're boarding. Sean likes to wait until the last call.

Sean loves to dream and think big. I'm a detail gal myself, thinking mainly week to week.

He stays up super late. I am sleepy by 9:00 p.m.

Anyway, I hope you get the idea. Can you imagine the two of us going anywhere together? Or successfully raising a family? Or doing life peacefully on a day-to-day basis?

Perhaps you are thinking, "Aww, that's too bad for you. My boyfriend and I are *exactly the same*." Well, Sean and I once thought we were *exactly the same* too. It is often our similarities that draw us into a relationship with a person, so those are usually the things we notice most while we are dating. No matter how much you feel like you are alike now, there are differences between you. They'll come out later.

Thankfully, we do have a few things in common. We both love God. We both really like each other, and we are both crazy about our kids. We both want to make disciples to reach all nations. We both like to read, and we both like Village Inn French Silk Pie. We agree on all of the important things.

As different as we are, we've learned to appreciate our differences, and together we make a pretty good team. We each bring different skills, abilities, and perspectives into our marriage, and we are both better because of it. Our differences in marriage make us better because "becoming one" with someone very different from yourself requires loads of compromise and self-sacrifice. Making those hard selfless choices to be unified in marriage with a spouse who is different from you, forces you to fight your selfish desires and learn to value others above yourself. The more you do this, the more you grow in Christlike character.

> *Be humble, thinking of others as better than yourselves.*
> *Don't look out only for your own interests,*
> *but take an interest in others, too.*
> *You must have the same attitude that Christ Jesus had.* [1]

An important aspect of appreciating differences is realizing that the qualities which attract us to someone can often become the very things which frustrate us most about them. Think of it as two sides of the same coin. When I am annoyed at Sean for parking the car crooked, thinking about the other side of the coin can help me appreciate the upsides of being married to someone so different from myself. The same man who doesn't care about the yellow lines in a parking lot, also doesn't care about a lot of unimportant things. His big picture focus balances my attention to detail and helps me keep things in perspective.

The differences you'll have can divide you or work to make you a stronger more balanced team. If you want an enjoyable and lasting marriage, it's important for you to understand and appreciate the differences people have. Two key ways you can grow in your appreciation of differences is to learn about personalities and love languages.

Appreciating Personality Differences

To keep life interesting, God made us all with different personalities. Having a practical understanding of these personalities can really help you understand yourself and relate better to the people in your life. It can help you now in your relationships with family members, roommates, and coworkers, and it can definitely help you later in marriage.

There are lots of personality profiles available these days—Myers-Briggs, the DISC inventory, and the Enneagram—but when I was in college, Florence Littauer ruled as Personality Queen. She published a lot of books based on four personality types—Choleric, Melancholy, Sanguine, and Phlegmatic. Here's a short, but telling, description of them:

Powerful Cholerics say "Let's do it MY way!"
Perfect Melancholies say "Let's do it the RIGHT way!"
Popular Sanguines say "Let's do it the FUN way!"
Peaceful Phlegmatics say "Let's do it the EASY way!"[2]

The funny thing is that early in my single years I told people I was a Sanguine, which is absolutely ridiculous. I apparently was very confused about who I was. No wonder

I spent those early years frustrated and worn out most of the time. I may have wanted to be a Sanguine, but I am actually the exact opposite. I'm a "textbook" Melancholy.

By the time Kathy and I were friends, I was beginning to realize this. When I finally met Sean, I was owning it and flourishing as a tried-and-true Melancholy.

Sean is a "textbook" Choleric. He's an incredible leader. He's confident in his decisions and always seems to know what to do. I admire his ability to connect well with people and inspire them. He's a visionary and always seems to be ready for the next thing.

If our relationship were a boat, Sean would be the sail and I'd be the anchor.[3] If our boat didn't have Sean, it would be really clean with organized closets, but we'd just sit in the harbor and never go anywhere. If our boat didn't have me, it would take trips all over the place, but it would be a mess and no one would have clean socks.

When you have team members with different skills and abilities, it makes the team better. When everyone is doing their thing, it helps the team overall. Being able to appreciate those differences will put you ahead of the game for sure.

Understanding Love Languages

Another area you can grow in as a single woman is understanding love languages. If your goal in marriage is to love your husband, it will be vital to understand how you each give and receive love.

When Dr. Gary Chapman came out with his book, *The Five Love Languages*, it revolutionized a lot of relationships. Everyone has a primary and secondary way in which they express and experience love. He explains there are five basic ways:

- Gift giving
- Quality time
- Words of affirmation
- Acts of service
- Physical touch[4]

God is merciful. You know why? Sean and I have the *same* love language! We both feel loved when we do acts of service for each other. When he does work around the house, I feel loved. When I do work around the house, he feels loved. Despite all our differences, just doing life normally, we naturally make each other feel loved.

Having the same love language as your spouse is actually rare. Often this is an area in which husbands and wives have to learn to understand differences between themselves and their spouse. We tend to show love in the way we want to receive love.

However, if the way you receive love is different from the way your spouse receives love, your efforts may not communicate the love you are trying to show.

For example, if his love language is words of affirmation and her love language is quality time, and they don't know that, they may have some struggles. He just wants to hear her say that he's doing a good job as a husband and dad, and he is probably saying affirming things to his wife in hopes that she will say some back. Meanwhile she may be planning activities for them to do together, not understanding why he doesn't seem to value these times like she does, and likely wishing her husband would stop telling her she's great and show her by planning a date night!

Welcome to marriage.

The good news for you is that you can learn more about

personalities and love languages ahead of time, while you are single. You'll be able to discover more about yourself and understand why you do things the way that you do. You can learn more about your friends so you can appreciate them and help them feel loved and understood.

If, when you are engaged, you and your fiancé go through premarital counseling, odds are you are going to talk about personalities and love languages. I'm saying, why wait? It is something you can totally start learning about now to get a head start.

Marriage has a crazy way of changing you. The longer Sean and I are married, the more we have become like each other. It's bizarre. Lately, our catchphrase is, "You've changed!"

Sean has become a fantastic planner and is much more attentive to details. I've kinda loosened up on the details. I'm dreaming big and taking risks like writing books and stuff. We've started boarding the plane at about the same time together. I've started enjoying hosting crowds, and I actually parked crooked the other day.

You can love your husband, before you even have one, by getting to know yourself better and learning to appreciate differences in your friendships.

Key Truth
Just as our bodies have many parts and each part has a special function, so it is with Christ's body. We are many parts of one body, and we all belong to each other. Romans 12:4–5

Points to Ponder
In what ways could a current relationship or friendship improve if you were able to better appreciate the differences between you?

Action Steps
Go to www.5lovelanguages.com and take the quiz to find out your love language.

Take a personality test and start learning about the different personalities.

Additional Resources
The Five Love Languages, Dr. Gary Chapman

Personality Plus: How to Understand Others by Understanding Yourself, Florence Littauer

Endnotes
1. Philippians 2:3–5.
2. Florence Littauer, *Personality Plus* (Grand Rapids, MI: Revell Books, 1983).
3. Not sure where I got this concept, but it isn't original with me.
4. Dr. Gary Chapman, *The Five Love Languages*, http://www.5lovelanguages.com/.

I had always thought time would heal old wounds. That I could let all my conflicts either resolve themselves, or one day I would just magically be over it. I've come to realize I was very wrong, and that my past is shaping my future in a not so positive way. If I can get better at resolving conflicts as they come, I'd have much more wholesome relationships with others and a less tainted heart.
— **McKenna, twenty-one, single**

———————

Learning to resolve conflict God's way has been a huge area of growth for me as a single woman. Because of the way I saw conflict resolved in my family and in the world around me, I grew up thinking conflict was bad and ruined relationships — even resulting in divorce. Once I began learning that conflict could be resolved in a godly, honoring, not yelling, not name calling, not giving the silent treatment way, it has drastically transformed my friendships and relationships with others.
— **Emily, twenty-nine, single**

———————

I knew my husband and I would have conflict. What I didn't expect was that we would both have to work hard for conflict resolution, and that it wouldn't be just him fighting for my forgiveness while I let him tell me how right and wonderful I was. I'm glad I practiced healthy conflict resolution before marriage so when the realities of marriage set in, I was better prepared.
— **Catherine, married three years**

———————

Conflict resolution? Never heard of it! I grew up in a family that vomited emotions with no regard for hurt feelings and then everyone just got over it. Needless to say, talking through frustrations isn't exactly my forte! But with practice, practice, counseling, and did I mention PRACTICE, God has blessed me with a healthy marriage!

— **Wife, married at twenty-six**

15

Milk vs. Cookies

Resolve Your Conflicts

Sometimes the transition from friends to roommates can be a game changer. Your relationship may be all fun and good times, but start living together and your differences come out. In the early years of roommate life, I simply avoided the conflicts. I noticed that ignoring the problems didn't really help much. If anything, the awkwardness and strain often made us both look forward to moving out. I was a terrible conflict resolver, but as the years and roommates went by, I got a little better at it.

By the time I married Sean I knew that I wasn't perfect at it, but I was committed to working through conflicts. It's a good thing, because we have definitely had our share of them.

One particular conflict was over milk and cookies. *For real.*

Years ago, when our kids were little, our family decided to go on a camping trip with some close friends. I say "camping" very loosely because we actually stayed in a cabin. Anyway, our two families divided up the responsibilities for the adventure. Since our family lived closer to the cabin site, it was my job to go to the grocery store and pack our food for the weekend.

Early that morning I got inspired and made a huge batch of chocolate chip cookies to take with us. After the cookies were all baked, I headed off to the store with my three little boys in tow. Now this may not seem like a big deal to you, but taking three little boys to buy a long list of groceries is not for the faint of heart. Ask any mom.

When we made it home, I pulled out our cooler and carefully packed it with all the refrigerated items, covered them in ice, and loaded the cooler in our minivan before everything else, because you always pack the big items first. Then I organized the groceries in bags and gathered all the miscellaneous items and packed them in, around, and on top of the cooler. Have I mentioned that I was doing this while keeping a watchful eye on three active boys? Trust me, that enhances the difficulty of any task.

As I was wrapping up the last bit of grocery packing, Sean made it home from work. Boy, was I glad he was home to help with the final preparations! He was pumped when I told him I had made some chocolate chip cookies. As soon as I shut the door on the minivan, he stepped out of the front door of the house with cookies in hand. "Hey Babe, did you buy any milk? We're out."

"Yes, I bought a few gallons for this weekend," I answered, "but I just loaded them in the cooler. They are buried in here under all the other groceries."

"Aw," he said with disappointment, "I was hoping to get some milk for these cookies."

"Babe, just eat the cookies without milk. You can drink some later. I *just finished* packing the car," I responded with a sigh.

Sean grew up in a home where they *always* drank milk with chocolate chip cookies, so he said, "But you can't eat chocolate chip cookies without milk."

I, however, grew up in home where we didn't have to have milk with chocolate chip cookies, so I said, "Yes, you can."

He shrugged his shoulders and said, "No, I really can't." Then, as if a light bulb went off in his head, he proposed, "Tell you what. I'll unload the groceries, get the milk, and then load it back exactly the way you had it."

Well, that wasn't what I wanted to hear. And with that, our conflict began. He couldn't understand why it would bother me for him to unpack the car to get the milk since he was going to do the work and repack it just the way I had it. I couldn't understand why he would flippantly unload the car for a glass of "unnecessary" milk when I had just worked so hard to get it all loaded in the car. We were both very frustrated with each other, and neither one of us could understand where the other person was coming from — all over milk and cookies.

That fun-filled family adventure began with some less-than-happy campers.

Conflict is what happens when
you disagree with another person about something.

Let's walk through this milk and cookie conflict

together, and I'll share with you the lessons I've learned about resolving conflicts along the way.

Lesson One: Conflict results from differences.

If you bring two people together, you will eventually realize some differences. Those differences tend to bring out disagreements, which lead to conflict.

Sean grew up always drinking milk while eating cookies. I didn't always have milk with cookies. Which way was right? Neither. One way was not right and the other wrong.

They were just *different*.

If you marry, you will have conflict with your husband. If you have a roommate, you will have conflict in that relationship too. People have different perspectives on things and do things differently. There are different ways to squeeze toothpaste, load the dishwasher, and place the toilet paper roll. And these are just the *smaller* decisions in life.

Lesson Two: Conflict is totally normal.

During my freshman year, when I didn't know many married people, I had class with a married girl. We often went to her house for our study groups because it was a no-brainer pick over everyone else's apartment or dorm room. One night, after we finished our group work, she said something I will never forget: "Oh my husband and I never fight. We never have any conflicts." I remember thinking, *Wow, that's awesome! That's the kind of marriage I want.*

Looking back, maybe she had only been married for a month or something, because I have since learned that conflict in marriage is *totally* normal—even in great marriages. It's actually the lack of conflict that is a bit odd, because it may mean someone is holding something in and not being completely honest about their opinions or feelings.

No two people agree on everything.

Lesson Three: Conflict doesn't necessarily mean fighting. The girl in my class was right in that conflict doesn't have to be a fight, as in yelling, screaming, stonewalling, and such.

Sean and I didn't start screaming at each other in our driveway over milk and cookies. We both expressed our frustration using a normal tone of voice. We couldn't understand where the other person was coming from, and not being understood had left each of us feeling hurt. I felt that Sean had been unappreciative of all the work I had done to shop and load the car while keeping three kids alive, and he felt that I was being unreasonable by not wanting him to unload the car to get milk when he offered to place everything back the way it was.

How you deal with such frustrations determines whether they become a fight or a healthy conflict. If you handle conflicts without turning them into an attack on the other person, resolving conflict can actually be a way for the two of you to grow closer.

Sharing with someone that you disagree with them can build trust in the security of the relationship. It's also important to note that what you truly believe about the other person will shape how you approach the conflict and communicate with them. If you believe them to be a good person who loves you and does not want to hurt you, you will approach the conflict with gentleness, anticipating resolution, and the relationship will be strengthened. On the other hand, if you do not trust or believe the best in the other person, communication can become attacking or defensive, and a conflict can more quickly escalate into a fight. In order to resolve conflicts without fighting, we must check our attitudes toward others before communicating.

Lesson Four: Resolving Conflict takes practice.

Learning to resolve conflicts is very doable while you are single. I had about twelve different roommates during my single years. Over time I began to learn that conflict wasn't necessarily a bad thing. Unresolved conflicts just led to more distance in my friendships. Caring for your friendships will push you to work through issues rather than just avoiding them. With all of my roommates, I had plenty of opportunities to practice my conflict resolution skills. By the time I had my first conflict with Sean, I wasn't perfect, but I had made a lot of progress in resolving issues with others.

Lesson Five: People handle conflict differently.

If everyone handled conflict in the same way, conflict resolution might be easier. But just as people have differences in personality and preferences, they also have differences in the way they approach conflict. There are three basic ways people deal with conflicts. Ideally, we should all try to be the person in the middle who handles conflict in the right way and resolves it. These people don't avoid it or make it a drama. They communicate and get it resolved. Although the middle ground is ideal, typically you will lean toward a "flight" or "fight" tendency when facing conflict.

Fight ◄————————*Resolve* ————————► *Flight*

Fighters don't back down from a conflict, and they fight to win. I am married to one. Sean is quick to speak his mind and is not afraid of a lively debate. Fighters need to learn to be patient and kind, even in the middle of a conflict, and to express themselves in a way that does not make the other person feel attacked.

Flighters would rather avoid conflicts and will do whatever it takes to keep the peace — even covering up what they really think or feel. I'm this one. Flighters might stuff feelings of hurt or anger, convincing themselves they can "just get over it." But stuffing feelings can lead to walls of resentment in relationships or eruptions of emotion when the flighter has finally "had enough."

Over the course of our marriage, we have both moved more toward the middle. One lesson that has really helped us is the "yellow light" concept, which is lesson six.

Lesson Six: Resolve conflict before it becomes a heated issue.

One key to managing conflict well is to take steps to resolve issues when you first start feeling something is wrong. Sean and I call that "yellow light" living. We began using the term when our boys were young and in the middle of nowhere one would yell from the backseat of the car, "I gotta pee RIGHT NOW!" We tried to teach them to let us know a little earlier, before the need became an emergency, so that we had a "yellow light" warning to start looking for a place to stop.

"Yellow light" means, instead of waiting until a conflict is a huge issue, we try to resolve these little irritations as soon as we notice ourselves becoming uncomfortable. For example, if your roommate is leaving dirty dishes in the sink and expecting others to clean them, it's best to mention it early and figure out a solution before it gets under your skin. If you wait too long, emotions build up and start spilling out, and it gets harder to resolve the issue.

Sometimes it may even mean that you have a roommate meeting to discuss your top three pet peeves. We all have them, so it may be helpful to just get them out in the open. We can't have everything exactly our way, but it is helpful when roommates work together to at least try to avoid each other's top three sources of irritation.

Lesson Seven: Don't let conflicts go unresolved.

When we allow a conflict to go unresolved, it doesn't go away. Every unresolved issue becomes like a brick, and bricks can build a wall between you and the other person. It's important to resolve each issue as it comes and not let them build up. Once a wall gets built between two people, it can be tough to restore peace between them because there are so many issues and negative feelings to deal with. Get in the habit of dealing with issues as they come up.

Lesson Eight: Try to enter marriage with as little unresolved conflict as possible.

If you are like most people, you currently have some unresolved conflicts. Sometimes we try to avoid the unresolved conflicts from our past, but ignoring them never makes them go away. They often come back stronger and more confusing than before and affect our current relationships. For that reason, it's important to go ahead and try to deal with any unresolved conflicts in your life so they don't get magnified in your marriage later.

Sometimes the walls in our hearts are a result of someone else's wrongdoing toward us. If there is any kind of abuse in your background, I would encourage you to start taking steps toward helping your heart heal from those hurts. I'll list some books at the end of the chapter that might be a helpful place to start, but it may be good for you to meet with a counselor to talk through past abuse as you move forward.

I'd also encourage you to try to resolve any issues you might have with your dad. As women, our relationships with our fathers often lay the groundwork for how we relate to men. This relationship can sometimes affect us more than we realize, and unresolved issues between a girl and her dad can pop up and become issues in a new marriage. Even if it seems impossible to be totally at peace with your dad, I would encourage you to do what you can to make things right. This may just mean that you go through forgiveness steps in your heart toward him.[1]

Lesson Nine: Get outside help if you need it.

In "The Great Milk and Cookie Conflict" we couldn't understand where the other was coming from. Even after talking on the drive to the cabin, we were at a standstill. We realized we had done all we could to try to resolve it on our own. We needed outside help and chose to involve the other couple we were camping with. Lucky them! When we arrived, we presented both of our sides. Our friends recognized that I felt unappreciated for all of the work I had done when Sean wasn't there, so they helped Sean understand where I was coming from. They also helped me understand Sean's perspective, that if he was willing to do the extra work to get the milk, I could have chosen to give up my preferences and let him do it, rather than feeling like I had to control the situation.

It's important when navigating conflicts to seek

counsel along the way from wise people, maybe parents, pastors/small group leaders, possibly even professional relationship counselors to better understand the other person's perspective. It is also important to learn how to communicate so you are listening effectively and being heard. It makes a huge difference in conflict resolution when people feel valued and listened to.

You want to hear something ironic? After twenty years of marriage, I have come around. I can no longer enjoy a chocolate chip cookie without a glass of milk.

You can love your husband, before you even have one, by learning to resolve your conflicts.

Key Truth
Do your part to live in peace with everyone, as much as possible. Romans 12:18 (NLT)

Points to Ponder
Are you a fighter or flighter by nature?

Action Step
Discuss the "yellow light" principle with your roommate and agree to implement it at the beginning of your next conflict.

Additional Resources
The Peacemaker, Ken Sande
There are many versions of this book—even comic books for kids! I recommend the student edition. It is an easy

read and very practical. In my opinion, it is the best book out there for learning about resolving conflicts.

Victory Over the Darkness: Realizing the Power of Your Identity in Christ, Neil T. Anderson
The forgiveness steps he lists in chapter 11 have been incredibly helpful for me.

For those who need to resolve sexual conflicts in their past:
The Wounded Heart, Dan Allender

Door of Hope, Jan Frank

In some cases, professional counseling may be needed, but these books can get you started in the right direction.

Endnotes
1. These forgiveness steps are listed in Chapter 11 of *Victory Over the Darkness* (Bloomington, MN: Bethany House, 2000).

I think girls see marriage as hanging out with your best friend all the time. Everything is equal, and you are supposed to pull your weight. There is no pressure on guys to lead relationships. Most guys my age haven't learned to lead yet, so girls think it's totally OK to be in control of the relationship and take pride in "wearing the pants."

—**Single girl, twenty years old**

———————————

When I learned this concept of love and respect, I'll have to admit, I was shocked! How does [everyone] not know this? The best thing I did for myself before I got married was first learning how to love and respect myself and become the woman God had created me to be. Now in marriage, I have such a better understanding of this from trying to apply it to my life long before my husband ever came around.

—**Megan, twenty-four, married at twenty-two**

———————————

I've always had a strong personality, and I naturally gravitate toward leadership roles. I love finding solutions to problems, and my assertive personality helps me execute my plans. When I heard that God's design for marriage was for a man to lead, I knew it would be a learning process for me. After several failed dating relationships where I was in the drivers' seat, I decided to trust God's design. I benefit every single day from marrying a godly man who leads our family so well. God's design really is best.

—**Meg, thirty-one, married at twenty-six**

16

Cracking the Code

Understand Love and Respect

I love Mexican food. So when Sean planned a nice date to eat Mexican food not long after he found out, I had a hint that maybe he liked me as more than a friend. At least I was thinking we were becoming more than friends, but he hadn't said anything yet.

Have you ever been in that awkward place between a friendship and a relationship? That's where we were, and I hoped Sean would bring up the "what are we" discussion during our date that night. Honestly, it was a bit tempting to just bring it up myself, but I was resolved that I would not make the first move.

Conversation flowed easily with Sean. I can't even remember now what we were talking about at the time, but as we were munching on our chips and cheese dip, I noticed that one of his shirt buttons was unbuttoned.

The fourth button down had been missed. It was gaping open, and it caught my attention. Now maybe that's no big deal for you, but I'm borderline OCD, and it was downright distracting. I debated in my head if I should say something to him, because I'm embarrassed to admit when stuff like that bothers me. But I couldn't stand it, so reluctantly I leaned forward and said, "Sean, can I tell you something?" He leaned in, smiling, and said, "Of course. What?" I sheepishly grinned, paused, and said, "You missed a button." A puzzled look came across his face, and he looked down and quickly buttoned his button. We both laughed, and a few minutes later he excused himself to go to the bathroom. I continued eating my chips, oblivious to what had just happened inside Sean.

I tried initiating in relationships before Sean, and it just didn't work for me. I like the way we did it better.

Later, after our relationship had been defined, he told me his side of what took place that night. Apparently he was thinking that we were becoming more than just friends too, but he secretly hoped that I would take the initial step of vulnerability and reveal my heart first. When I leaned forward in such an odd manner and said I wanted to tell him something, he was gearing up for me to expose my feelings for him. When I didn't say what he was expecting and instead brought up a random button, it threw him off. He then had to excuse himself to process it all. Away from the table, he was disappointed in himself that he had wanted me to initiate. He decided right then that he would take the lead in our dating relationship. He later told me, "As much as I wanted you to take the risk first, I was glad that you didn't. It pressured me to step up." Then he said this: "Even though I wanted you to initiate, if you had, I would have felt like less of a man."

On our next date, Sean took me on a picnic, told me that he liked me, and asked if I would date him exclusively. (I said, "Yes!" by the way.)

Years later I was back at the very park where Sean and I became "a thing." I began to share our picnic story with the women there with me. My dreamy reminiscings were interrupted as they began to pummel me with questions: "Why did he have to be the one to initiate things in your relationship?" "Why didn't you just tell him how you felt?" "Why did you have to wait on him to do that?"

I should have expected their questions. In all honesty, there was a time when I would have asked the same questions myself. Maybe you just asked them too. I simply responded by saying, "I tried initiating in relationships before Sean, and it just didn't work for me. I like the way we did it better."

So why did I like this way better? Isn't it old-fashioned and counter-progressive for a woman to want a man to lead a relationship?

I grew up thinking it was the girl's job to help a guy out by letting him know she liked him first. However, every time I did initiate with a guy, even if he responded positively, I felt a twinge of disappointment. I kept initiating with guys, even though it didn't feel quite right, because I believed it was the only way to get a guy's attention. If I didn't help a guy out, how in the world would I ever get a date or have a boyfriend?

As I got older, I watched godly men pursue women. I began to see a different way, and I liked what I saw. One young man, who treated his wife incredibly well while they were dating, told me once, "If a man really likes you and wants to spend time with you, he won't need any help to ask you out." I wanted to be pursued like that. Along with that advice, a woman I really looked up to challenged me: "Let God put love in a man's heart for you." I liked that too. I was tired of trying to fight my way into a guy's heart. Another man I worked with and respected told me, "Kim, there will be times in marriage when a husband needs to know that he started the relationship." I admired each of these friends' marriages, so their advice was convincing. I was sold.

I felt honored and respected by the initiative Sean took in our relationship. I enjoyed being pursued without having to help him out. I liked that he would make the drive to my town in an effort to come to see me. I liked that he planned our dates. I liked that he came to the door to get me. I liked that he opened doors for me and paid for my meals. I liked that he took the responsibility to communicate with me. By taking initiative to pursue me in these ways, he communicated that he was putting time and effort into this relationship because it mattered to him. You can go ahead and call me old-fashioned, but I liked how that man made me feel.

What Sean felt was respect and admiration when I let him lead, and I felt cherished and loved by his pursuit.

I was tired of passive guys. I was tired of the confusion they caused. Were they going to step up or not? Did they like me or not? They'd act like they were interested, but then they'd never say anything. Later, I'd hear they were with another girl! I was tired of guys who would spend time with me only to say, "So what do you want to do?" They either *didn't know how to lead* or *they didn't want to*, and it was confusing and unattractive.

I was looking for a man who took the initiative to lead and guide a relationship. I was willing to not take control to see if Sean would lead. He did lead, and he did not disappoint.

The Mexican-button scenario revealed some innermost desires in both of us. When I let Sean lead and communicated how much I admired his leadership, it made him *feel* like a man. When he initiated in our relationship and pursued me without my help, I liked how it made me *feel*. We both liked those feelings, and as it turns out, what we were wanting in our dating relationship actually corresponds to how God designed marriage to work.

Sean and I didn't have specific terms at that time for the feelings we liked, but what Sean felt was respect and admiration when I let him lead, and I felt cherished and loved by his pursuit. Isn't it interesting that the Bible instructs husbands and wives in the following manner?

Each man must love his wife as he loves himself,
and the wife must respect her husband.[1]

These specific instructions God gives His followers actually meet the unique desires we naturally have inside of us as men and women. God made us, so He knows how we work best. As we have talked about in earlier chapters, there are some needs only God can meet, but there are other needs He specifically wants husbands and wives to meet for one another: A husband needs to love his wife as he loves himself, and the wife needs to respect her husband.

Here's how these ideas play out in marriage: When I allow Sean to lead in our relationship, and I express sincere appreciation for his efforts to do so, I meet the deep desire in him for respect and admiration. As I show this to him

by my words and actions, it stirs up his love for me. As
Emerson Eggerichs explains in his book *Love and Respect*,

*The best way to love a husband is to show him respect
in ways that are meaningful to him. Such respect lets
him feel his wife's love for him and ignites in him
feelings of love for his wife.*[2]

When Sean continues to pursue me and prioritize our
relationship, it meets my deep desire to feel loved. It stirs up
respect and admiration in my heart for him. Eggerichs says,

*Psychological studies affirm it,
and the Bible has been saying it for ages.
Cracking the communication code between husband
and wife involves understanding one thing:
that unconditional respect is as powerful for him
as unconditional love is for her.
It's the secret to marriage that every couple seeks,
and yet few couples find.*[3]

Unconditional love is a concept we are probably familiar
with. However, we usually think of respect as something
that is earned rather than given unconditionally. The idea
that wives are to show respect to their husbands out of
obedience to God rather than in response to their husband's
actions is often a difficult concept to wrap our hearts and
minds around. It is important as women that we realize
our respect communicates to men the same relational
acceptance and devotion that their love communicates to
us. It is also important that we learn to recognize when a
man feels disrespected, so we can begin to identify words

or actions that might cause him to feel that way. Eggerichs tells us how to crack the code:

Whenever a wife is complaining, criticizing, or crying, she is sending her encoded message: "I want your love!" And whenever a husband is speaking harshly or sometimes not speaking at all, he is sending his encoded message: "I want your respect!"[4]

A man's response to feeling disrespected can often appear to us as an eruption of unexplained anger. If he cried as a response to disrespect, we would likely feel compassion toward him; however, his anger may make us defensive or judgmental. In your current relationships with males (boyfriends, coworkers, fathers, brothers) begin to take note of how men respond when they feel disrespected. Not only can gaining this awareness improve the way you relate to the men in your life, but it will prepare you to better understand how to meet your future husband's deep needs for respect.

When Sean and I are regularly meeting each other's deepest desires, it makes our marriage thrive. The key to continuing to thrive, however, is that we are each committed to do our part *unconditionally*. This means that Sean *chooses* to love me, even if I am not lovable or respectful at the moment. Likewise, I *choose* to be respectful toward Sean, even when he might not be meeting my expectations, and when I do not feel love from him.

These hard choices we make again and again to put

If you know what's ahead, you'll prepare and marry more wisely.

our spouse's needs ahead of our own are the key to how we keep winning each other's affections back. All this is called unconditional love and respect, and frankly it's very hard to do. Although we are each committed to doing our part no matter what, we are far from perfect at this. We desperately need God's help to do it. When we get it right, our relationship flourishes and things between us just seem to click. When we fail to meet each other's needs, it causes hurt and frustration, and we have to work together, communicating and forgiving, to get things right between us again.

One of the primary reasons marriages fall apart is that couples continually fail to meet each other's core needs.

Unfortunately spouses all too often think, I will do my part, if and only if, my spouse is also doing his/ her part. Could this be one of the main reasons that so many marriages aren't working very well? I think so. Unconditional love and respect are a critical component of a happy, lasting marriage. For that reason, I believe it is especially important for you to understand the deepest needs of husbands and wives *before* you are married, preferably *before you even choose who to marry*. If you know what's ahead, you'll prepare and marry more wisely. You'll be ready.

Going into marriage with an understanding of love and respect helps you meet each other's needs from day one, setting your relationship up for success.

Because love and respect are so foundational to healthy relationships, getting this dynamic in place from day one of your marriage establishes the right type of patterns. Meeting each other's core needs builds and deepens trust and intimacy in your relationship. On the flip side, couples that start off without an understanding of love and respect may damage trust and intimacy in their marriage unknowingly by failing to meet their spouse's primary needs. This damage to the relationship can cause unhealthy patterns of isolation and mistrust, building walls of hurt in the marriage. Understanding love and respect before you go into marriage starts you off on the right foot to overcome one of the biggest obstacles to healthy relationships.

The initial pattern Sean and I started in dating followed us into our marriage.

Creating a marriage that meets each other's core needs requires a partnership with a mate who is on the same page. If you marry a guy who doesn't understand what God wants him to do, it will still fall to you to give him the admiration and respect he needs.[5] May I be honest? It is very difficult to respect and admire a man you really don't respect and admire. I'd much rather have this conversation with you as a single woman, than to have it with a wife who doesn't feel loved by her husband and doesn't respect him.

Even if he's cute and good-hearted, a guy who constantly needs others to do things for him or isn't successfully managing his own life, won't be so cute if he becomes your husband. A girl might hope she'll be able to change him once they marry, but that doesn't work well. A guy is usually "at his best" when you are dating—he is trying to win you! If you are marrying him thinking he will gain more initiative, or become way more romantic, you will probably be disappointed. Trying to change him will likely make you frustrated and leave him feeling disrespected and eventually resentful of you. Let that guy develop more on his own before you intertwine your heart with him. You should marry a guy "as is."

If he's not the type of man you would see yourself naturally respecting or wanting to partner with "as is," then maybe he isn't the one for you, or now is not the right time.

The initial pattern Sean and I started in dating followed us into our marriage. He has continued to take the lead in our relationship. Now, as my husband, he takes the initiative to make sure our emotional, spiritual, and financial needs are met. As his wife, I continue to cooperate with and respect his leadership. We will never be perfect at these roles no matter how hard we try. As I mentioned before, executing unconditional love and respect is hard, very hard! However, each year we get better at meeting each other's deepest desires, and our relationship has steadily grown stronger.

On a related note, it's hard to lead well. Most men don't have dads who modeled it for them. Being a leader is tough and tiring. Recently Sean walked into the room after making a decision that wasn't popular with our teenagers. He was kidding, but he laid on the bed and said, "I just want to be passive like other guys out there. It would be so much easier."

To which I responded, "No way! I like it better when you lead. I'm so grateful for you. Please keep leading us!"

If you want to marry a man who will take initiative in the important areas of life, you should look for a man who demonstrates leadership in your dating relationship.

You can love your husband, before you even have one, by understanding how love and respect work and how this design meets the desires of a husband and wife in marriage.

Key Truth
So again I say, each man must love his wife as he loves himself, and the wife must respect her husband. Ephesians 5:33

Points to Ponder
Have you felt frustrated or confused in relationships with passive guys? Do you think there is a better way than taking the initiative yourself?

Action Step
Instead of taking control when a guy is passive, choose not to initiate to see if he is willing and able to lead.

Ask the men in your life (dad, brothers, boyfriend), "What does respect look like to you?"

Additional Resources
Love and Respect, Dr. Emerson Eggerichs
This is must read if you want to be married someday. Failure to understand this concept is one of the main reasons I have seen so many marriages fall apart, and you won't hear this message much in our culture.

Rocking the Roles: Building a Win-Win Marriage, Robert Lewis and William Hendricks

Endnotes

1. Ephesians 5:33.
2. Emerson Eggerichs, *Love and Respect* (Nashville: W Publishing Group, 2004), 19.
3. Eggerichs, inside cover.
4. Eggerichs, 40.
5. Ephesians 5:33.

I really struggled with believing that the man I always dreamed of could actually be out there and assumed I was just destined to settle for something less. But I'm sure glad I trusted God to let go of "good" guys that walked my way and waited for "he exists, and he's mine!" God knows each of us better than we know ourselves, and isn't going to call you to a life of higher standards when it comes to relationships to leave you dry. He will provide exactly what you need in ways you couldn't have picked better yourself. Trust God, pursue His mission for your life, and watch what He does.
—**Hannah, twenty-six, married two years**

The pressure felt overwhelming. Every holiday, family event, or birthday prompted questions of, "Are there any prospects out there? Are you dating anyone? How are you still single?"
In those moments, it was hard to communicate why I was so selective when considering a mate. And honestly, it was hard to remain selective. But I was always grateful for the one voice of reason, my grandpa, who always chimed in with a reminder "Wait for a man of character who loves God and chooses Him first." I have to tell you, I'm so glad I followed his advice and God's advice because I married a man of character who loves God and chooses Him first, and I can't imagine it any differently.
—**Alyssa, twenty-six, married five months**

I had always known good character was important in someone I would date and marry, but a mentor explained to me that godly character is everything. Two years into marriage I am more convinced of this every single day. My willingness to follow his leadership, my respect for him, my personal growth and even my confidence in our relationship are each directly affected by his integrity and depth of character. My best decision, second only to trusting Christ, was marrying a man with godly character. I am reaping the benefits of that decision daily.
—**Alex, twenty-eight, married two years**

17

Kings and Queens

Choose Him Wisely

One afternoon in the car I was steaming mad and venting to Sean about it as he was driving. A husband we both knew had been a jerk to his wife, and I had just found out about it. His words to her were rude, and his actions were immature. I was shocked and basically went off to Sean about this guy's lack of character. I went on and on about it as Sean drove. Eventually Sean turned to me and said, "You know, Kim, you're right. He's been a total jerk…" As he turned back to face the road again he added, "but she *chose* to marry him." I huffed, crossed my arms, and stared out the window at the trees going by. That's when I decided to add this point to my material.

You didn't get to pick out your mom. You didn't get to choose your dad. You didn't get to pick your siblings either.

You didn't get to choose anyone in your family. You just get the family you get. The good news is *you* get to shape your future family. *You* get to choose who you marry. *You* get to pick your husband. *You* are the one who chooses the dad for your future kids. It's *your* decision.

It's a lot easier to love your husband if you choose a good man to begin with. If you want to love your husband, before you even have one, choose your husband wisely.

What do I mean by *wisely?* My old-school pocket dictionary defines it as:

1. having good judgment.
2. informed or learned.[1]

> It's a lot easier to love your husband if you choose a good man to begin with.

Judging something basically means you make a call on it, as either right *or* wrong. Not everything or everyone is good for you. Wisdom is what helps you decide that.

When you choose a husband, you need to be wise. You'll need to discern if he is the best man for you. If you are going to choose a Mr. Right, you need to know what's true and right, and the Bible is a great place to look for wisdom.

Fear of the Lord is the foundation of wisdom.
Knowledge of the Holy One results in good judgment.[2]

My working definition of what it means to "fear the Lord" is to care more what God thinks than what anyone else thinks. Fearing God doesn't mean I'm scared of Him, but I do treat Him differently than everyone else. I like this definition:

*Fearing God means having such a reverence for Him
that it has a great impact on the way we live our
lives. The fear of God is respecting Him,
obeying Him, submitting to His discipline,
and worshipping Him in awe.*[3]

The Bible says, when we know God well, and He has His rightful place in our lives, we're in the best spot for gaining wisdom and good judgment. In this book we've talked about *Know God Well* and *Put God First*. Those are steps you can take toward God that will help you to become wise.

The opposite of being wise is being foolish. A foolish man is one "lacking the maturity to be discriminating… easily deceived."[4] It reveals "a low development or deficient use of reasoning abilities."[5] You get the idea.

We see the difference between a wise and foolish person when Jesus compares them in Matthew 7:

*Therefore everyone who hears these words of mine and
puts them into practice is like a wise man who built his
house on the rock. The rain came down, the streams rose,
and the winds blew and beat against that house; yet it
did not fall, because it had its foundation on the rock.*

*But everyone who hears these words of mine and
does not put them into practice is like a foolish man
who built his house on sand. The rain came down, the
streams rose, and the winds blew and beat against that
house, and it fell with a great crash.*[6]

The wise man and the foolish man both heard Jesus' words. They both faced exactly the same storms in life. The difference was the wise man put Jesus' words into practice, and the foolish man didn't. The end results were vastly different. The wise man's house stayed standing, but the foolish man's house fell with a great crash.

If you want an enjoyable, *lasting* marriage, I hope that you will not shut God or His words out when you are making decisions about who to date and marry. You need to hear God's words and put them into practice. It will help you wisely choose a husband and build a marriage that will survive the storms of life.

Here's another bit of truth about wisdom.

Walk with the wise and become wise;
associate with fools and get in trouble.[7]

Find people whose lives you admire and ask for their perspective on situations and relationships in your life.

I hope you will also surround yourself with wise people. If you spend time with people who know how to live well, then it will rub off on you. If you hang out with foolish people, their influence will rub off on you too. That's how it works. Because of this truth, I think it is important for you to start building relationships with wise people now so they will be there along the way as you make decisions in your relationships. It's always good to have many advisers in your life. The book of Proverbs tells us:

Without wise leadership, a nation falls;
there is safety in having many advisers.[8]

Advisers are like rearview mirrors. They can see things from another perspective and can keep you from crashing into something you may not have noticed. I am so grateful for the opportunities I had in college to connect with some older believers through our campus ministry, and I am thankful for the church family I was a part of as a student. Find people who are following God and doing relationships well. Spend time with them. If you don't have people like this in your life, ask God to help you find some. Campus ministries and local churches are a great place to start the search.

Often, young women see the importance of asking others for advice, so they turn to their friends. Asking a friend for help with relationships may feel safer than approaching a woman at church, but a friend may not be able to offer the wise perspective you need. Sometimes our friends have the same perspective we do, which keeps them from being great "rearview mirrors" for us. Our peers often lack additional wisdom and life experience beyond what we already have. For this reason, it is good to not just ask your friends for advice, but to also have older people you can trust for counsel. Find people whose lives you admire and ask for their perspective on situations and relationships in your life.

When seeking wise counsel look for someone who:

- is putting God's Word into practice.
- has a life and relationships you admire.
- has learned from mistakes they have made.
- is ahead of you in life experience.

When Sean and I started spending time together, we had older couples who took an interest in our relationship. They asked us questions and offered advice. A few of my guy friends who were husbands stepped in like big brothers and spent time getting to know Sean. We had individual accountability with mentors to help us stay pure sexually. We had people "in our business," and I am so grateful for them.

I also hope you will involve your parents. I used to think my parents didn't know me or understand the things I was dealing with, so I rarely sought their counsel. Now that I'm a parent, I realize my thinking was very foolish back then. I have known my kids their *whole* lives, and I do know them quite well. I have also lived a lot longer than they have and wrestled through many of the same decisions they are making. We've coached them since they were little to invite advice from us as they pursue relationships. Even if God and His Word don't play a strong role in your parents' lives, I hope you will still seek their insights. This is even a great way to honor your parents and strengthen your relationship with them.

We chose each other wisely, and it has made all the difference!

Since my heart had been hurt a few times in relationships, when Sean asked me to date him I had a request. Call me old-fashioned, but I wanted him to talk to my dad first.[9] Sean wasn't asking me to marry him, he was just asking if we could date each other. But I wanted him to involve my dad even at this early stage in our relationship. Sean drove to visit with him the very next day.

I'm sure my dad was a bit confused at first, but once Sean explained that he just wanted to involve him in our process, my dad rose to the occasion. Literally. There's a reason why I am six-foot-one—my dad is six-foot-six. When he was visiting with Sean, he looked at him seriously and said, "Sean, don't you hurt my daughter." I appreciated my dad's protection of me, and was glad to know Sean had some big motivation to handle our relationship well.

Next, Sean wanted me to go out to Colorado to meet his parents. Apparently they approved, because on our way back from that trip, Sean asked if I would be willing to spend time with some godly older married couples to start discussing topics as we explored the possibility of marriage.[10]

All this wisdom and counsel may seem like a lot of work, but it paid off. Sean and I entered marriage with minimal surprises. We had talked through almost everything before we walked down the aisle, and we are so grateful for those who cared enough about us to help us start marriage well. Now as we face issues in our marriage, we have other couples we can turn to for help. We put the work in on the front end. We chose each other wisely, and it has made all the difference!

You should get input from wise people when choosing a husband, but ultimately it is your choice. There are a lot of guys out there to choose from. There are even a lot of good guys. So how do you choose?

Say there's this guy. You have fun together, listen to the same music, and your friends think you make a cute couple. You could just keep hanging out like this forever, but you wonder if it's going anywhere. Even though you enjoy your time with him, you need to figure out if this is a guy you could ever actually marry. So how do you know if a fun guy you like spending time with could be a potential future husband?

Here is a list of questions that I hope will help you think about whether or not a guy is "marriage material." You may even want to ask your parents or mentors to help you evaluate a guy you are considering based on these questions.

Qualities to Look For

Do you admire his relationship with God?
How long has he had a relationship with God? Did he have one before he met you? Is it an integral part of his life or just something he does on Sundays? Does he pursue his own spiritual growth, or is he dependent on your promptings?

Is he intentional with you?
Do you feel like a priority in his life? Does he make time for you? Does he communicate consistently?

Is he teachable to other men?
Having a man who learns from other men will reap benefits in your future marriage. Does he have a mentor? Does he ask older men for counsel?

How does he handle his emotions?
Is he able to control his anger? Does he shut down easily, become pouty or withdrawn? Does he resolve conflict? Forgive others?

Does he protect you?
Does he value your purity? Does he guard your reputation by keeping you out of questionable situations? Does he put you down or insult you in front of others? Do you feel safe with him? Does he ever scare you?

How does he treat his parents and siblings?
Anyone can act like a gentleman to impress you, but how does he treat the people who already love him? How a man treats his mom is often a good indicator of how he will treat his future wife.

Do you like his friends?
Those who are closest to us shape us the most. Do you like their character and the influence they have on him? Does he act differently around his friends than he does when it's just the two of you?

How does he handle money?
In what ways has he shown financial responsibility? Is he in debt? How does he feel about debt? Is he generous?

Does he show leadership around other men?

Leadership isn't a position or title—it's influence. One of the best ways to tell if a man will be able to lead his family someday is if he is leading other men now. Is he taking initiative in others' lives? Is he well respected by his peers?

Is he kind?

How does he treat servers at restaurants?
Do your family and friends like the way he treats you?

Does he keep his commitments? Is he truthful?

Marriage itself is based on a commitment. If he's faithful in the small things, he'll more than likely be faithful in the big things. Can you trust what he tells you?

Is he a hard worker?

Does he take initiative to successfully manage the details of his life (job, school, cleanliness), or does he need help or prompting?

Does the Bible have authority in his life?

Does he make decisions based on what the Bible says or based on what he wants? There's nothing like his view of sex before marriage to reveal if God's Word truly has authority in his life.

How does he view his mistakes?

Has he repented of mistakes in his past? Has he learned from them? Is he pursuing different choices now?

How does he handle sexual temptation?

Does he take steps to get out of tempting situations? Does he try to avoid them to begin with?

How has he handled porn? Drugs or alcohol?

An addiction won't just go away when you get married. Does he joke about porn with his friends? Is he careful about what he chooses to look at? Does he have a successful track record of fighting against it? Does he misuse any substance?

Does he respect the authority in his life?

Does he rebel against authority in his life? What is his relationship with his parents? It will be much easier to respect your future husband if he is a respectful man himself.

Now, here's a question for you:

Would a man with these qualities you are looking for be looking for a woman like you?

That's a kicker, isn't it?

Sean and I often refer to the concept that *like attracts like*. People who work out are usually not attracted to couch potatoes. People who are well educated don't typically fall for high school dropouts. See what I mean? So, if we want to marry a king, we need to be a queen.

The good news is, as you are making the choices we have talked about to live wisely, develop your gifts and skills, grow in your relationship with God and learn how marriage works, you are becoming a queen. You are growing into the type of woman a guy with royal standards would hope to marry.

I know you may be wondering if there is even such a guy out there, but there is. He may still be in process right now, growing and developing, so you might not notice him yet. He'll be like you, wondering if the kind of girl he hopes for really exists. And if marriage is part of God's plan, then God will bring you together, and you will have your own stories to share of His faithfulness. Until then, focus your efforts on the choices you can make and the things you can do now to build your future wisely, and wait expectantly for God to amaze you with what He does when you trust in Him.

You can love your husband, before you even have one, by choosing him wisely.

Key Truth

The wise woman builds her house, but with her own hands the foolish one tears hers down. Proverbs 14:1 (NIV)

Points to Ponder

Where do you go for advice on relationships?

Action Step

Identify some godly older believers whose advice you would value. Introduce yourself.

Endnotes

1. *Webster's New World Pocket Dictionary*, 1977, s.v. "wisely.".
2. Proverbs 9:10.
3. Gotquestions.org, "What does it mean to have the fear of God?" https://www.gotquestions.org/fear-God.html.
4. Gary Hill, *The Discovery Bible* s.v. "moros," (Chicago: Moody Press, 1987), 530.
5. Hill, 530.
6. Matthew 7:24–27 (NIV).
7. Proverbs 13:20.
8. Proverbs 11:14.
9. My mom had passed away a few years before. I'm sad that Sean and my mom never had a chance to meet each other.
10. Sean and I went through some pre-engagement counseling and after we were engaged we went through pre-marital counseling, which also included some financial counseling.

Therefore everyone who hears these words of mine and puts them into practice is like a wise man who built his house on the rock. The rain came down, the streams rose, and the winds blew and beat against that house; yet it did not fall, because it had its foundation on the rock.

But everyone who hears these words of mine and does not put them into practice is like a foolish man who built his house on sand. The rain came down, the streams rose, and the winds blew and beat against that house, and it fell with a great crash.
—**Matthew 7:24–27** (NIV)

Conclusion

Happily Ever After!

After my first engagement ended, I became convinced God had a better way of doing relationships, and I wanted to find out how. I've been growing and making mistakes since that day, and along the way, I've learned some things. I found out how, and I came back to share it with you.

Throughout this book I've been telling you stories of how I have tried to put God's Word into practice in my life and in my relationships. I hope it's been helpful. I definitely haven't been perfect at it, but thankfully Jesus said "into practice" and not "into perfection."

As we go through life, we can either ignore what Jesus says or we can put those things into practice. Jesus says if we put His words into practice, our lives will still be standing when the storms of life hit. If we ignore what He has to say, our lives will crash when those storms come.

I know you are surrounded by others making choices all around you right now. You are probably watching couples fall in love left and right. Many of them are building their relationships foolishly, without a care for what God says, and they seem happy. They aren't putting God's Word into practice, and it doesn't seem to have any negative effects on their life at all. Emotional boundaries? Godly character? Fighting for purity? Judging from what you see around you, it can all seem irrelevant right now. Everywhere you look you see couples living foolishly who appear to be doing just fine.

Jesus says if we put His words into practice, our lives will still be standing when the storms of life hit.

As a single woman your age trying to live wisely, I really struggled with this. *God, how come you ask me to make all these decisions that are hard, yet everyone else who is living foolishly seems to be doing just fine? I mean, what difference does it really make?*

Have you ever shared that struggle?

Well, here's something I wish I had understood earlier:

The consequences of making foolish choices and the rewards of making wise choices usually don't happen right away; they often come later in life.

Right now you are making choices, but you aren't seeing the outcome of those choices. Give it ten or more years. When you get older like me, you see some of the outcomes.

Have you ever cried with a wife who married a man who didn't treasure sexual purity? I have.

Have you ever had a wife confide in you that she's scared her husband is cheating on her? I have.

Have you ever had someone ask you when to tell a fiancé about an STD? I have.

Have you ever heard the struggle of a wife dealing with the fallout of her husband's porn addiction? I have. She was crying so hard I could barely make out her words.

Have you ever answered the phone in the middle of the night and heard a wife scream that her husband just left her? I have.

Have you ever counseled a wife whose marriage was struggling because she didn't share her husband's life purpose? I have.

Have you ever seen an affair and two divorces result from a "friendship"? I have.

Have you ever heard a bitter wife say, "I will NEVER forgive him." I have.

Have you ever heard the struggles of a woman who was married to a man she no longer respected? I have.

Have you ever cried with a woman who still had emotional pain over an abortion she had in college? I have.

Have you ever tried to explain to a wife the importance of respecting her husband when she felt no love from him? I have.

When a woman comes to me and the consequences of her life are crashing down around her, I want to help, but usually the damage has been done, and there are no quick fixes. I'm often at a loss as to what to say that could help her, and that really bothers me.

Then I go home to Sean. You know all of those "hard" choices I made when I was single? Well, they paid off. We have faced a few significant storms already—life storms that have split other couples—but we're still standing. We've taken some hits, but we still like each other. As I cry and hurt for those I care about, Sean holds me and reassures me of his love and commitment.

> *It's been in those teary, broken moments that I have resolved in my heart to say something.*

It's been in those teary, broken moments that I have resolved in my heart to say something. I may not always have the words to say to those I care about who are struggling in their marriages, but to those who aren't married yet, I know exactly what to say. And that's how the material for this book, *Loving Your Husband Before You Even Have One*, was born.

When I see young women making decisions I know might damage their future relationships, only to see the culture around them cheering them on, well, it just breaks my heart. I had to speak up and say something.

As you know, I've made my share of mistakes too. Probably many of the same ones you have made. Christ gives us hope, and our past mistakes don't have to define our future. As a young woman, Jesus gave me a chance for a new start.[1] He offers this to you too. I'm grateful for the hope He gave me. I'm also thankful I was young enough to make some significant changes in my life. As long as we are breathing, because of what Christ did for us, there's hope for change.

Life is messy, and there are no guarantees to get a husband or formulas for a perfect marriage. Relationships involve two people, and we can't control others' decisions. I don't know if Sean will always follow the Lord and make wise choices, and he has no guarantees on me either. If he were to flip out and walk away, I'd still be thankful I made the choices I've shared with you. If I had never been given a husband, I would still be glad I made these choices. God has given us commands and principles to live by. If I am building my life by putting God's words into practice, then I can trust the promise that I'll be able to hold together and withstand the storms.

Your single years are a rare and precious time that you should make the most of. Don't waste these years pining for what you don't have. Instead, enjoy what you do have! You have a God who wants a relationship with you. Get to know Him and enjoy what He has done for you.

Your single years are a rare and precious time that you should make the most of.

He made you for a special reason, and He has a purpose for your life. This life is so short, and we can start investing in the lives of others to make an eternal difference. You don't have to be married to get started on that. Discover your purpose and find fulfillment using the unique gifts and abilities that He's given you. See what God can do through you.

Don't wait to start your life until you get married. Grow, learn, prepare. Hang out with your girlfriends, travel, eat good food, and most importantly, work on becoming the best version of yourself. Enjoy these years you have to invest in you, your future, and the lives of others.

Discovering who you are and finding your fulfillment in the God who made you will bring abundance to your single years and prepare you to love your husband, if you marry. Live on purpose and build your own happily ever after starting now!

Oh yeah, and someday when you end up with stories of God's goodness and faithfulness to you, don't forget to go back and share them with the younger women around you.

**You CAN love your husband,
before you even have one!**

---

*The wise woman builds her house,
but with her own hands the foolish one tears hers down.
Proverbs 14:1 (NIV)*

Endnotes
1. 2 Corinthians 5:17.

Acknowledgments

I never realized how much of a "team sport" writing a book is, but this book simply wouldn't exist without the people listed below. As a result of this experience, I will never, ever skip over reading an acknowledgment page in a book again.

Sarah Billings, my unofficial editor, your eyes saw this material first. If you hadn't cheered me on, I might have chickened out. Grateful for you and your friendship!

Heidi Loften, you were there when I was single. You were there when Sean and I were dating. You were there the night we got engaged. You were there at our wedding. I doubt many writers can say that about their editor. Thank you for sharing the heart behind the book and for going over each word on every page. A big piece of you is in here too, and it is a better book because of you.

Sarah Scott Pape and Kaitlyn Osborn, you're in here too! Thank you.

Adrienne Bloomer, you made everything look better than it should have.

Shad, thank you for investing your life in college students. My life is different because of you.

To the older women who taught me the things I wrote about: Kathy Brown, Carol Shadrach, Julia Robinson, Michelle Rofkahr, Karen Nelson, Evelyn Stillwell, Brenda Burnett, Trish Carruth, and Sandy Brown, you opened up your hearts and homes and allowed me to enter in and learn from you. I am deeply grateful.

To my focus team of fellow StuMo staff and students: Meg, Jena, Hannah, Meagan, Becky, Haven, Mary, Melina, Val, Hallie, Megan, Christen, Lacey, Brittany, Macie, Molly, Kim, Alyssa, Laura, Brooke, Kara, Krista, Amanda, Allie, Sarah, Kelsey, Cat, Alyssa, Catherine, Tonya, Abbey, Madison, Morgan, Deven, Maddy, Natalie, Kenzi, Eva, McKenna, Tori, Cymber, Madi, Alyssa, Maylee, Dotty and Anna, thank you for your perspective and input to make this book more clear and relatable.

Dad and Mary Kay, thank you for caring for me when I camped out on your couch to write. Double Honor Ministries, many of these chapters were written in your beautiful lake home. Thank you for sharing it.

Fisher, Sim, and Stone, thank you for enduring a distracted mom and eating a lot of sandwiches over the past few months. I'm praying it will all pay off when you attract and marry a woman who loved you beforehand.

Sean, I love doing life with you. Thank you for making this book happen.

The Good News

I f we were able to hang out and have coffee together, I would love the opportunity to talk through Romans 6:23 with you. Although I am not sitting across the table from you, if you'll grab a cup and a quiet spot, I'd like to share something with you. The message in this verse is good news, and it changed everything for me.

For the wages of sin is death
but the gift of God is eternal life
in Christ Jesus our Lord.
Romans 6:23

For the **wages** of sin is death...
When I think of wage, I think of minimum wage. Is that what comes to mind for you? A wage is something we earn.

For the wages of **sin** is death...
How would you define sin? Behind all the sins we might list out, there's an attitude of rebelling against God or just ignoring Him. Sin is disobeying God, and we've all disobeyed Him in one form or another. Me included.

For the wages of sin is **death**…
This verse says that sin has earned each of us death. If this meant physical death, I would have been dead a long time ago. It's referring to a spiritual death or separation from God. God is without any sin, so our sin separates us from Him. Have you ever felt this separation?

…but the **gift of God** is eternal life…
A gift is completely opposite from the wage we talked about earlier. A wage is something we earn, but a gift is something given to us. A gift is not earned. This verse says that God gives this gift.

…but the gift of God is **eternal life**…
This verse says that the gift God gives us is eternal life. Eternal life is a relationship with God that will last forever. It's the opportunity to know and be known like I talked about in Chapter 9. It's the life we crave. It's the opposite of death or separation from God. Even though we've sinned and have earned death, He gives us eternal life. *Pretty amazing.*

…**in Christ Jesus** our Lord.
Eternal life is in Christ Jesus. As we've talked about, our sin was separating us from God. When Jesus died on the cross, He took our place and died the death our sins had earned us. But Jesus didn't stay dead. He came back to life and opened up a way for us to have eternal life—a relationship with Him that will last forever.

…in Christ Jesus **our Lord**.
The Bible says it is not enough to just believe this is true. Each person must individually receive the gift God has

given. We must receive Christ for who He is. Christ is called "Lord" in this verse. A lord is someone who is in control. To receive this gift of eternal life in Christ, we must turn from our sin. We must trust in Christ's death and resurrection for forgiveness of our sins, trust in Him to be our Lord and let Him take control of our lives.

You heard my story about how I turned from my sin in Chapter 2 "Experience God's Forgiveness" and how I trusted Jesus to be Lord in my life in Chapter 3 "Put God First."

Would you like to receive Christ?

If this prayer expresses the desire of your heart, you may receive Christ right now.

"Lord, I admit to you that I am a sinner and that I am separated from you. Thank you for wanting a relationship with me. Thank you for sending Jesus to die on the cross for my sins. I want to turn from my sin and trust Jesus Christ to forgive me and take control of my life. Please make me into the person you created me to be.
Amen."

If you make this decision, let me know at kim@kimvollendorf.com

I'd love to pray for you and pass along some encouragement and resources to help you grow in your relationship with Christ.

Standing at six-foot-one, Kim Vollendorf is literally a "big sis" to younger women. For over thirty years, she has served with the campus ministry, Student Mobilization. She is a wife and mom now, but she is well acquainted with being single. She enjoys a nice cup of tea, a good read, a hearty laugh, and a well-organized closet. She and her husband, Sean, have three sons. Keep up with her on instagram at @sixonesis and at her website www.kimvollendorf.com.

Kim donates a portion of proceeds from sales of this book to International Justice Mission and to Student Mobilization.

International Justice Mission (IJM) is the world's largest international anti-slavery organization, working to fight modern day slavery, human trafficking, and other forms of violence against the poor. Learn more at www.ijm.org

Learn more about Student Mobilization at www.stumo.org

Additional Resources

The *Loving Your Husband Before You Even Have One* podcast allows Kim to continue the discussion alongside her younger co-host Adrienne and their wise, insightful guests. You will hear from others about choices you can make now to flourish during your single years and increase your odds for an enjoyable, lasting marriage later!

Loving Your Husband Before You Even Have One

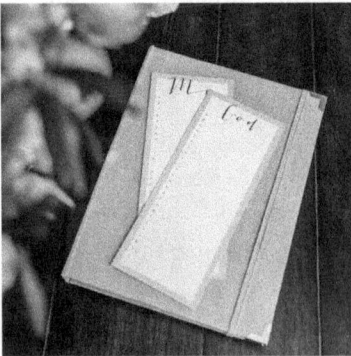

In addition to Kim's Instagram @sixonesis, www.kimvollendorf.com has other resources and freebies. She is in the process of developing new materials, and you can stay up to date as they come out by subscribing to her email list.

From Kim's Husband

Kim's husband Sean is the host of a podcast by aspiring men, for aspiring men. In today's culture, achieving manhood as our Creator intended is elusive, It's rare. This podcast exists to get the godly man off the endangered species list.

THE ENDANGERED SPECIES

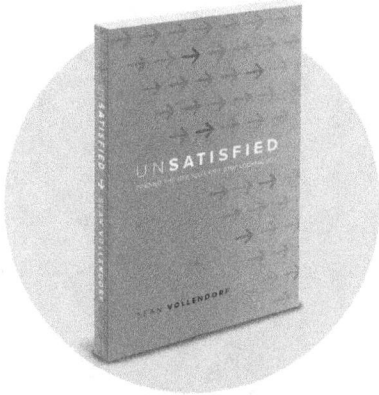

Whether we consciously know it or not, we're all looking to be gratified, to feel fulfilled. With everything that's available to you in this world, will you find satisfaction? Find Kim's husband's book and more at www.compress.org.

www.ingramcontent.com/pod-product-compliance
Lightning Source LLC
LaVergne TN
LVHW052019080426
835513LV00018B/2081